FREEDOM BEYOND WEALTH

The Blueprint to Wealth, Abundance and a Purpose-Driven Life

BY

JUSTIN COOK

Ordering Information: Quantity sales. Special discounts are available on quantity purchases by corporations, associations, and others. Orders by U.S. trade bookstores and wholesalers.

Contributor - Kelsey Menchaca

DREAMSTARTERS

www.DreamStartersPublishing.com

Table of Contents

Introduction

Embracing Failure and Finding Purpose

If you're someone who tends to open a book but never quite gets around to finishing it, let's start with the first lesson now: it's okay to fail. In fact, it's more than okay—it's necessary. It's okay to take risks, make changes, and even go all in when your heart tells you it's the right thing to do. Looking back, it was failure, along with the willpower to persevere through adversity, that led me to where I am today.

In this book, my goal is to share that journey with you. I hope that in reading my story, you'll find value for your own life—whether it's a lesson that helps you develop habits for success, a new strategy for building wealth, or a bit of inspiration to leave your own legacy. This is a roadmap, drawn from both the successes and the failures I've experienced, and it's yours to make use of.

Nice to Meet You

My name is Justin Cook, and I grew up in Cape Girardeau, Missouri. I was raised with my mom, dad, and sister, and my childhood memories are so vivid that sometimes they feel like they happened just yesterday. There are mornings when I swear I can smell my mom's biscuits and gravy drifting through the house, only to realize it was just a dream. Cool November mornings remind me of heading out to a deer stand with my dad, while the glow of baseball field lights on a summer evening brings me back to the pitching mound, feeling the dust rise with each pitch.

These moments weren't just scenes from my childhood—they were the experiences that shaped my life. They instilled a sense of purpose, a foundation of values, and a competitive drive that's stayed with me. Through sports and family, I learned the thrill of improvement, of putting in the work to win, both as part of a team and on my own. My parents invested countless hours supporting my practices, my games, and everything in between. For that, I am deeply grateful.

Now, I have the absolute joy of watching my own children, Hudson and Lola, discover and fall in love with their passions. Lola is my beautiful, creative, and thoughtful girl. When she's not hustling on the volleyball court, she's out in nature, drawing, catching frogs, and letting her imagination soar. Hudson, on the other hand, is a fierce competitor—a little lion with an eagerness to win each day. If he's not outside shooting hoops, he's watching basketball, talking about basketball, or counting down the minutes until he can get back to "shooting hoops." Watching them grow and express themselves is one of the greatest privileges of my life, and I am so proud to be their dad.

Why This Book Matters

This book isn't just a collection of business advice or personal anecdotes; it's The roadmap that's brought me to where I am today. Each chapter will walk you through the experiences that have shaped my journey, from the moments of failure to the milestones of success. I'll share how I've positioned myself in the insurance industry and why I'm passionate about what I do. I'll open up about the lessons I've learned—lessons about resilience, purpose, and building a life and career that feel meaningful.

Whether your goals are in business, personal development, or legacy-building, I hope that you'll find something within these pages that speaks to you. The journey to success is rarely a straight line, and it's often the setbacks, challenges, and unexpected twists that teach us the most. My hope is that by sharing my own roadmap, you'll feel inspired to draw your own.

So, let's dive in. As my son Hudson would say,

"Let's go!"

Part 1

The Inside Game

Chapter 1

Rejection

"Rejection is part of the journey toward success, so don't be insulted or get upset when it happens. In fact, get excited about how you just got closer to your 'Yes!'"

Michelle Moore

Learning to overcome rejection has been one of the most crucial lessons in my life and is ultimately one of the reasons I am successful today. My hope for you, reader, is that when you're faced with the word "no," you keep moving forward with your head held high. If I had let those "no's" defeat me, I would likely still be working the same position I had in college, stuck at the bank and probably miserable.

If you have a dream, hold it close and let no one discourage you. When you have a vision, take massive action to bring it to life! In this chapter, I'll share my own journey from athletics to career and explain how I overcame being rejected six times before landing my first agency role. I'll also provide some tips at the end for using rejection as a tool for growth. Now, let's dive into the journey of rejection—let's go!

Falling in Love with Baseball

My love affair with baseball began when I was just six years old. For me, the thrill wasn't just in playing the game; it was in preparing, practicing, and pushing myself to get better every day. Games were just the icing on the cake.

When I took the mound, I gave it everything I had. During game days in high school and college, I was focused to the point where I hardly talked to anyone. My only goal was to bring my best—for myself and for my team. Through middle school, high school, and into my early college years, my life revolved around pitching. Every ounce of my energy went into becoming the best pitcher I could be.

But as my time in the game wound down, I knew I needed to channel that same energy and dedication into something new. The passion and commitment I had for baseball would need a new outlet.

A Shift to Career Focus

Growing up, I took on side jobs here and there, dabbling in different “businesses.” One of my early ventures involved selling rabbits door-to-door with my best friend, Josh Miller, for $2.50 apiece. Sometimes we branched out, selling turtles or even blackberries. Those side gigs taught me the basics of business, but eventually, I had to take on a more traditional job.

My first “real” corporate role came while I was still in college—I worked for a bank. Just as I had with baseball, I brought dedication and focus to the job, determined to learn and grow every day. Working at the bank was a new experience for me, and I treated it with the same drive I’d shown on the baseball field.

As I gained experience, I started to visualize my future at the bank. I pictured myself climbing the corporate ladder, reaching for that elusive light at the end of the tunnel. But the longer I thought about it, the more I began to realize that I might be headed down the wrong tunnel. Even if I made it to the top, I didn’t think it would bring me true happiness. That realization sparked something in me—it was time to reevaluate.

Seeking New Paths and Mentors

Who do I want to become?" It was a turning point, and a light bulb went off in my head. I knew I needed to explore other options and learn more about different industries.

To gain insights, I arranged meetings with people in a range of fields. I spoke with two investment advisors, three insurance agents, and three bank presidents. Each meeting provided valuable information that helped me better understand my options. I was grateful for the time these professionals shared with me and for their willingness to pass on their knowledge.

One conversation, however, stood out from the rest. This was with a bank president who ended up giving me advice that would change the course of my life. During our meeting, I asked him if there was anything he would change about his career path. He paused, then thoughtfully admitted that if he had to start over, he would have chosen a different path.

He explained that, if given a second chance, he would have become an insurance agent. He believed the career offered a more flexible schedule and a higher income potential. That answer hit me hard. Here was a successful bank president telling me that he would have rather been an insurance agent? That revelation sparked my interest, and I knew I had to look when I realized that banking might not be my future, I started asking myself some big questions. “What do I really want?” “What do I need?”

Taking the First Steps Toward a New Path

Now that I’d decided to pursue a career as an insurance agent, it was time to dive in and get to work. I knew I needed more information, so I thought about who else I could talk to. Suddenly, it hit me—one of my good friends Justin Shelby’s dad worked in the insurance industry. I gave my friend a call, and soon enough, his dad welcomed a conversation about his experience.

After learning more, I felt fully confident in my decision to pursue a position as an agent with a major insurance company. That confidence reminds me of my own daughter, Lola. She’s an avid frog catcher, and she’s been fascinated by frogs since she was a little girl. We have a stream in the backyard, and one of her favorite evening activities is to head out by the stream to hunt for frogs as the sun sets.

Before Lola goes “hunting,” I’ll often ask her how many frogs she thinks she’ll catch. She’s quick to give me a number, and her confidence in hitting that “frog count” is absolute. She doesn’t stop until she’s reached her goal! That same confidence and determination that I see in Lola was exactly how I felt about my decision to join the insurance company. I’d made my choice, and now, the real journey was about to begin.

The Application Begins: Testing the Fit

My first step was making contact with the insurance company. I quickly learned that becoming an agent wasn't as simple as filling out an application and waiting for a response. They had high standards, and put a lot of effort into ensuring they select only those who are truly suited for the role. I appreciated that level of commitment; it made me respect the process even more.

The Path Forward: Education and Planning

The next step took me to Columbia, Missouri, where I attended an educational meeting with others interested in becoming insurance agents. This meeting was another crucial step in the process. After the meeting, the company would decide which candidates would be invited to continue.

The day after the meeting, I received a call—I was invited to move forward. The excitement was overwhelming. Step two was checked off the list, and I was ready for what came next.

This new phase was all about business planning and assessment. The company required each candidate to create a detailed business plan covering key aspects like building a team, marketing an office, serving clients, managing finances, and setting achievable goals. Over the course of three months, I put my all into developing a thorough plan. This was my future, and I was determined to make it great.

The Big Presentation

The final test was presenting my business plan in front of eight people in a boardroom in Columbia, Missouri. That morning, I was as focused as I'd ever been—similar to how I'd prepare for a big game back when I played baseball. Before a high-stakes game, I'd isolate myself with my headphones on, listening to pump-up songs like "Eye of the Tiger," one of my all-time favorites. My teammates knew that this was how I prepared mentally, and it helped me get into the zone.

That morning, I used the same approach. I zoned in, clearing my mind and focusing solely on the task ahead. When I walked into the boardroom, I felt a combination of excitement and nerves, knowing that this presentation could determine my future. Finally, I was able to present my plan, and I felt a huge wave of relief when it was over. I hoped that I'd done enough to impress the board and earn an interview for an open agency position.

So far, I had attended the educational meeting, met with agents, prepared a detailed business plan, and presented it. Each step brought me closer to my goal, but now, all I could do was wait. Two days later, I received the call.

A Setback with Step Three

Step three remained unchecked. They told me I wasn't ready to move forward in the process. Naturally, I felt disappointed, but I wasn't about to let this be the end of my dream. I had a vision of becoming an agent, and I was willing to do whatever it took to get there. Instead of giving in to discouragement, I opened my mind to their feedback. They suggested that I build up my finances and gain experience by working for a agent. I took their advice seriously.

Soon, I started working for Mike Jones in Cape Girardeau, Missouri. I'm grateful to Mike and for everything I learned during my time in his office. Those experiences were instrumental in preparing me for the next steps. Mike knew from the start that my ultimate goal was to become an agent myself, and he was supportive of my journey. After 18 months of working under Mike's guidance, I returned to that same boardroom with a healthier balance sheet and real experience from within a company office.

This time, the outcome was different. I had taken their feedback and put it to work, and it paid off. Step three, check! I was finally eligible to interview for opportunities with open agencies. When I got the news, it felt like landing a big buck in the fall—a perfect blend of excitement and satisfaction.

The Search Begins: Chasing Opportunities

With step three complete, I immediately started looking for agency opportunities in my hometown of Cape Girardeau, Missouri. Unfortunately, the company didn't anticipate any openings in or near Cape Girardeau for at least two years. Patience has never been my strong suit. I was ready to take the leap, and I wasn't about to wait around for two years. So, I expanded my search and began considering agency openings across the USA.

My first pick? Brandon, Mississippi. When I say I was willing to look anywhere, I mean it—I was 25 years old and ready to interview 392 miles from home. I prepared intensely, getting into my zone as I would for a big game. But this time, I wasn't pitching; I was stepping up to the plate.

The First Interview: Brandon, Mississippi

Game day arrived, and I felt calm, prepared, and confident. I approached the interview like a batter stepping up to face a pitcher. I watched that first "pitch" come in and took my swing. Unfortunately, it was a slider I hadn't anticipated. Swing and a miss, strike one. Interview one, Justin zero.

I didn't make the cut in Brandon, but that was just the beginning. Although the result was a "no," I treated it as an opportunity to learn and refused to let it discourage me. I had already come so far, and I wasn't going to give up just because I missed the first pitch.

Second Interview: Nashville, Tennessee

Two months later, I had my second shot—this time in Nashville, Tennessee. I took what I'd learned from the Brandon interview and showed up in Music City eager, determined, and more prepared than before. I wasn't aware at the time that over 30 candidates were vying for the same agency opportunity.

Despite my preparation and enthusiasm, I struck out again. Interview two, another "no." This time, the rejection stung a bit more. With each setback, the pressure mounted, but I didn't let it break me. Once again, I took their feedback, made a list of areas for improvement, and got to work. I focused on building my finances, honing my leadership skills, and seeking out the next opportunity.

Third Interview: St. Louis, Missouri

My third opportunity came up in St. Louis, Missouri, "the Gateway to the West." I was thrilled at the prospect—St.

Louis was closer to home, and as a lifelong Cardinals fan, the thought of living in that city felt right. Maybe there was a reason the first two interviews hadn't worked out. This one felt like it might be meant to be.

The day of the interview, I felt like I was up to bat with two strikes already against me. I was ready to either hit a home run or strike out swinging. The pitcher threw a curveball to the outside, and I swung—another miss.

Three interviews, three rejections. I was somewhat awestruck. Despite all the rigorous preparation and dedication, I still hadn't landed an agency. But rather than letting this third "no" knock me down, I took it in stride. I listened carefully to their feedback and used it as fuel to become even better. I was more determined than ever to be so prepared that when the next opportunity came along, I'd be the clear choice.

Fourth Interview: Centralia, Missouri – "The Anchor City"

My fourth attempt brought me to Centralia, Missouri, known as "the Anchor City." By this time, I was fully invested in my goal. I even visited Centralia a few times before the interview, getting a feel for the town. I took my mom out to breakfast there, picturing myself living and working in this community. I felt certain I was ready for this position and believed I was the best candidate.

This time, I approached the interview with renewed energy. When I sat down to interview, I was reminded of my baseball days, still up at bat with two strikes against me. The interviewer threw the first "pitch" right down the center, but I hesitated, cautious. I let it pass—strike one.

Interview four. My fourth "no." It's hard to express the emotions I felt after that fourth "no" in a row. It reminded me of a similar feeling hunting whitetail deer one November many years before.

One crisp fall morning, I climbed up to my deer stand, settled in, and waited. Hunting gives me time to reflect on life and business, especially when I'm alone. There's something about being out in nature, with nothing but the quiet sounds around you, that clears your mind. That morning, as I sat deep in thought about the week ahead, a young buck wandered into view. Now, let me tell you—no matter how big or small the deer, I get excited every single time. My girlfriend can tell you firsthand how intense it gets. She nearly has a heart attack every time I yell "DEER!" while driving, especially when I spot a buck. She often thinks we're about to get into an accident with how loud I get. But when it's hunting season, that excitement just comes naturally.

But back to the story. I decided to pass on this particular "DEER!" The buck was young, and I wanted to give him time to grow. So, I waited. An hour later, I heard movement in the trees. The sound of leaves rustling and the distinct blow of a deer caught my attention. I froze, watching and waiting. The first thing I saw was a glimpse of antlers emerging from the trees, and as he came into view, I realized this guy was a shooter. He was about 90 yards away—far enough to make it a challenge, but close enough to be hopeful. I took my crossbow, steadied myself, and released the arrow. Missed it.

Not a great feeling. I waited a couple more hours before climbing down from my stand to retrieve my arrow. When I reached it, I was shocked to see blood on it! I immediately called my dad, who was hunting in a different area on the farm, to tell him I'd hit the buck after all. Together, we trailed the blood for three hours. But, as time ticked away, I had to leave to attend an Iowa basketball game with my family. By that point, I wasn't feeling too optimistic; I figured the deer was long gone.

That sense of disappointment—that feeling of coming so close only to fall short—is the best way I can describe how I felt after my fourth interview. It was the most significant letdown I'd felt in the process so far, but even then, I hadn't lost hope. I was ready to try again.

Fifth Time's the Charm?

My fifth pick for an agency opportunity was in Eldorado, a town located in southern Illinois. This time, it was down to just two candidates, meaning I had a 50/50 shot. For the first time, I felt like I was on the verge of a breakthrough. After all the “no’s,” I was ready for a “yes.” I was back up to bat, and this time, I felt like my odds were finally in my favor.

As I walked into the interview, I was focused and prepared. I felt like I was in the batter’s box, waiting for the first pitch. The pitch came, I swung, and I made contact—this time, it felt like I’d really hit the ball. I took off, rounding first base, pushing forward with everything I had. But as I approached second base, I heard the unmistakable sound of the ball landing in a fielder’s glove.

Out. Again.

Interview five, another “no.” This time, though, the rejection came with a silver lining. Along with feedback, the company offered me the opportunity to become an intern. It wasn’t the full agency role I’d been chasing, but it was a foot in the door, a step closer to where I wanted to be.

I accepted the internship position and stayed in that role for six months, gaining even more experience and learning from the inside. When an agency opening came up in Mt. Vernon, Illinois, I knew I had to go for it. At last, there seemed to be a light at the end of the tunnel. Maybe, just maybe, this would be the “yes” I’d been waiting for.

The Sixth Interview – Another “No”

The sixth interview for an agency opportunity arrived. Once again, I was one of only two candidates up for the position. Walking into the interview, I felt cautiously optimistic—50/50 odds felt promising. I stepped up to the metaphorical plate, waiting for the pitch. The first one passed by, and I let it go. When the second pitch came, I swung and made contact, sending a grounder straight up the middle. But just like that, I was thrown out at first.

Six interviews, six "no's." The disappointment was weighing on me, but I still wasn't willing to give up. I continued working as an intern, trying to stay motivated and regroup. Three months passed as I kept my head down, focused on improvement, and waited for another opportunity.

A Call from the North

One morning, while sitting at a office in Chester, Illinois, my phone rang. The voice on the other end was Randy Coon, a sales leader from northern Illinois whom I had never met. His opening words immediately caught my attention: "Word is you like to hunt and fish, and I have the perfect agency opportunity for you."

Intrigued, I asked the obvious question: "Where is this opportunity?" This sounded like the break I'd been waiting for, but part of me wondered what the catch might be.

Randy went on to explain that the opportunity was in Aledo, Illinois. I quickly googled "Aledo, Illinois" and discovered that it was a small town in a rural area, seemingly in the middle of nowhere. Aledo, with its population of around 3,500, was famous for its annual "Rhubarb Fest" and surrounded by fields of corn and beans stretching as far as the eye could see.

Randy invited me to come visit, and I agreed. I drove six hours north to spend a day in Aledo, getting a feel for the town. Its quiet charm and open fields resonated with me, and after speaking with Randy and seeing the area, I decided to go for it. I would interview for the seventh time.

Game Day: The Seventh Interview

This time was different. Randy had called me and invited me up, which made me feel hopeful. But I knew other candidates were also vying for the opportunity in Aledo, so the stakes were still high.

Once again, I found myself up to bat. Bases loaded, pressure on, and my batting average wasn't looking great at this point. I zoned in, determined to make this one count. Pitch one—a slider. Ball one. Pitch two—fastball down the middle. I swung with everything I had.

The ball went soaring into right field. I took off, watching it fly. Going, going… gone. **Grand slam!** That ball was out of there.

Later that day, I received the call I'd been hoping for. I had finally hit my mark. The agency was mine. After two years of trying, failing, regrouping, and improving, I had done it. Aledo, Illinois—my new beginning.

A Moment of Triumph – Never Giving Up

The excitement I felt was indescribable, but there was one moment that came close to capturing it. Remember that story about the deer I thought I'd missed? The one I spent hours tracking, only to leave the search unfinished that night? Just like with the agency, I hadn't given up hope. I returned to the woods the next morning at 5 a.m. with my dad, and together we tracked for two more hours until, finally, I saw the deer's antlers on the ground. We were jumping up and down, thrilled at the sight of it.

That's exactly how I felt when I got the call from the company, confirming I was their choice to be the agent in Aledo, Illinois. Both moments are memories I will never forget.

After all the highs and lows, the setbacks and small victories, I finally got a "yes." If I hadn't failed, I wouldn't have learned. And if I hadn't learned, I wouldn't have succeeded.

So, remember this: don't be afraid to fail. Each "no" brings you closer to your "yes."

Keep Shooting, Keep Dreaming

My son Hudson has a passion for basketball and spends hours each day shooting hoops in the driveway. Can you imagine if he gave up every time he missed a shot? If he quit the game altogether after each miss, he'd never improve, never experience the joy of making that perfect shot. That's how I approached each interview: like shooting hoops. I knew that if I stopped trying, I'd never score. I could have let the first rejection stop me in my tracks, but I didn't.

With each interview, each setback, I became stronger and more equipped for the demands of business ownership. I kept "shooting the ball," kept "hunting for frogs," kept "tracking the deer"—never giving up hope, always getting better, always moving forward.

Key Takeaways

1. **Rejection Is a Stepping Stone:** Each "no" is an opportunity to grow and improve. Embracing rejection helps you become stronger and better prepared for future challenges.

2. **Keep Your Goal Clear and Visible:** Having a clear vision keeps you focused and motivated, even when the journey gets tough.
3. **Adapt Your Path, Not Your Vision:** Sometimes, success requires adjusting your approach. Stay flexible and open to change, but stay true to your end goal.
4. **Perseverance Builds Resilience:** The ability to keep moving forward, no matter how many times you fall, is what separates those who succeed from those who give up.
5. **See "No" as a Chance to Improve:** Use each rejection to learn and refine your skills, making you even more prepared for the next opportunity.
6. **Surround Yourself with Positivity:** Seek out those who encourage you to keep going and lift you up during setbacks. A positive support system makes the journey easier.

Prompt for Reflection

How can you use a recent "no" as a chance to improve and grow? Are there areas in your life where persistence and flexibility could bring you closer to your goals?

Final Thought

Every "no" brings you closer to a "yes." Let each rejection be a chapter in your story of resilience, pushing you to become stronger, wiser, and more prepared for the opportunities that lie ahead. Embrace rejection, and let it be the fuel that drives you to success.

Chapter 2

Risk

"Life is inherently risky. There is only one big risk you should avoid at all costs, and that is the risk of doing nothing."

Denis Waitley

My dreams don't have limits, and neither should yours. To get from where you are to where you want to be, risks are necessary. Maybe you've already taken some and are now aiming for the next level! For me, I'll keep taking risks to keep moving forward. In this chapter, I'll share some of the risks I've taken and explain why risks are not only beneficial but essential. I'll also discuss the importance of trusting your instincts and being brave.

Finally, I'll share simple tips to help you prepare for taking risks and facing failure.

Learning to Thrive Under Pressure

When I think of facing pressure, I remember a story from when I was twelve years old, unsurprisingly related to baseball. At that time, my team faced a powerhouse team from Kentucky. They were intimidating—they showed up to games with matching backpacks, synchronized warmups, and a fierce dedication. They weren't just good; they expected to be good, every time they stepped on the field, they expected to win.

The next year, in 1995, I was invited to play for that Kentucky team I'd always admired. This wasn't just any team; it was a chance to play alongside players who set the bar high. The opportunity came with a risk. The coach had high expectations, and I knew I'd be commuting three hours to practices and traveling across the country to play. I questioned myself: What if I joined and couldn't handle the pressure? People around me asked the same thing, "What if you fail?"

But instead of letting fear dictate my decision, I asked a different question: "What if it works?" I didn't let the possibility of failure keep me from taking the leap. I committed, knowing it could be an incredible opportunity.

Embracing the Pressure

Once I joined, it was game on. I trained hard—three hours in the morning and three more in the afternoon, every day. Looking back, I'm thankful I did. Baseball has always been more than a game to me; it taught me to raise the bar, to thrive under pressure, and to perform. I learned that life will always have moments of high stakes, so set your expectations high and step up and swing the bat!

The lessons I learned on that team became invaluable later in life. Baseball taught me the value of taking leaps and helped prepare me for another big decision that was yet to come.

The Leap to Aledo

Fast forward to that life-changing phone call from the company about the agency in Aledo, Illinois. I'd finally received my long-awaited "yes," and now it was time to make a decision. The company had offered me the position, but accepting it meant uprooting my life and moving 358 miles from Cape Girardeau to a small, rural town where I knew no one. A town that had seen two agents come and go in six years.

Excited, I shared the news with family and friends. Many were thrilled, but some expressed concern. I understood their hesitation. They worried about the risk: "What if it didn't work out?" But just as I had with baseball, I reminded myself: "What if it does?" The thought of failure wasn't enough to keep me from taking this leap.

So, I jumped. Within two months of accepting the offer, I was living in Aledo, immersing myself in the community's culture. My goal was to build my reach and help as many people as possible.

Reflecting on the Journey

When I opened the doors to my new office in Aledo, I realized just how valuable my experiences working for six different agents had been. Each "no" along the way, each rejection, had prepared me in ways I hadn't anticipated. Those experiences gave me confidence, resilience, and the knowledge that I could handle whatever came my way.

Looking back, I'm grateful for every rejection, every challenge. Each one built my staying power, my willingness to never give up. Failure, it turns out, is one of life's greatest opportunities for growth.

A Wake-Up Call – The True Value of Protection

With the experience I gained from working in insurance, I also developed a deep passion for protecting families with life insurance. Here's why.

Two months into my first position at an insurance office, I met with a 47-year-old contractor, married with three children all under the age of ten. His wife was a stay-at-home mom, and they'd recently built a new home together. During our meeting, I asked him one crucial question: "What would happen to your family if you didn't make it home tonight?" His response was honest and sobering—without his income, his family wouldn't be okay, and they didn't have any protection in place if something happened to him.

We went through a life insurance needs analysis, which showed he needed about $1,000,000 in coverage to protect his family fully. We both agreed on this amount, but when it came time to move forward, he hesitated, saying he "needed to think about it." I followed up with him twice, but he was still thinking it over.

Then, one morning, I walked into the office, and the agent asked if I had been working with this man. I explained that I had met with him, done the analysis, and recommended coverage, but he hadn't committed yet. The agent's response left me speechless—the man had unexpectedly passed away in his sleep.

If he had just signed that policy, his family would have had the financial support they needed. They could have paid for final expenses, stayed in their home, maintained their income, and funded their children's education. But without it, I watched his young widow struggle financially to raise her three children, eventually having to sell their home.

The Mission to Make a Difference

This experience changed my career forever. I realized I couldn't apologize for advocating for a solution that people needed. I should have been more assertive, more proactive. That day, I transitioned from being in the insurance business to being in the education business. I learned that I had a moral obligation to ensure families were protected.

If you're reading this and know you need life insurance, stop procrastinating. Write the check and take care of your loved ones, because you never know when your last day is. This became my "why." This experience and mission are why I took the risk to put everything into becoming a agent, even if it meant moving to a town where I knew no one.

Settling into Aledo – A Leap of Faith

Moving to Aledo was the biggest risk I had taken in my life. It's a small town, and at the time, I was 25, the third agent there in six years. Many people doubted I would stay, asking, "When are you going to be leaving?" The last two agents hadn't lasted, so people assumed I wouldn't either. Building trust and relationships took time, and early on, I felt like I had a lot to prove.

The office I inherited was on a dead-end road, set back a few blocks from Main Street. It shared a building with a hair salon. The visibility wasn't great, and space was limited. But none of that mattered. I was committed to my dream, even if the road was rocky at first.

A Moment of Determination

One memory from those early days in Aledo stands out vividly. I was attending a lunch at the local county fair's chamber meeting when a local insurance agent walked up to me, shook my hand, and said, "Welcome to your competition." He handed me his business card and added, "In case things don't work out for you."

In that moment, I could feel my commitment solidify. I'd moved 358 miles to be here, and I knew I wasn't going anywhere. As I left the chamber event, one thought kept repeating in my mind: "I will make a difference." I wasn't about to let skepticism or competition derail my purpose. I had a vision, and I was here to see it through.

The Impact of Taking Risks

Over the years, I've taken plenty of risks that have truly made a difference. I've invested in a wide range of marketing platforms, from billboards and radio to print ads, social media, and everything in between. Some worked wonders; others didn't. But each was part of my effort to expand my reach and share my purpose with the community. At the end of the day, I wanted people to know my name and understand why I do what I do.

One of the bolder marketing moves I made was plastering a large image of my face on cars driving down the interstate. It may sound surprising, but it worked! Those cars with my face on them have become driving billboards, making impressions on people who might otherwise never think twice about insurance.

In a small town, this generated plenty of buzz, some of it positive, some of it skeptical. But as I always say, "it makes you look, even if you don't want to!" I closely monitor my marketing's effectiveness, and I'll continue to invest and take risks that make an impact. It's all about staying visible and never settling for "okay."

Building the Right Team

Another significant risk has been growing my team. Hiring is like setting off a row of dominoes—you hire one, then another, and soon you're always looking for the next one. My goal has been to build a team that's equipped to provide the best support for individuals and families. That said, hiring is one of the most challenging parts of leadership. When you set high expectations, finding people who match your level of commitment can be tough.

I've made some great hires, and I've made some bad ones. I coach my team hard, believing deeply in our mission and ability to help others. Every day, I ask myself, "How can I change more lives?" This keeps my "why" front and center, motivating me and my team to push harder.

Investing in a New Office

I moved to Aledo in 2008, and from the start, my dreams were limitless. By 2011, I was ready to invest in building a new office on the busiest road in town. It was a major upgrade from the small office I'd been sharing on a dead-end road. Many people questioned my decision, seeing it as a risky move to pour so much money into building an office. But I took the leap, and we broke ground.

Building that new office wasn't just about having a better space; it was a step forward in my journey to grow and serve more people. Every time someone questioned my choices—to move away, to put my face on vehicles, to post on social media, to build that office, or eventually, to open a second office—I chose to move forward. Taking these risks was essential to reaching my goals and living out my purpose.

Lessons Learned from Risk and Failure

There will never be a perfect time to take a risk, make a change or pursue a dream, it is important to have a vision and a plan, but you'll never know every detail ahead of time. Don't let fear of failure hold you back from your potential. The most critical thing to remember when facing your fears is to avoid becoming your own worst enemy. Don't create unnecessary anxiety or hold yourself back before you even start.

Failure is part of the process. The only thing that matters is how you respond when you do fail. If you're not facing any failures, then you may not be dreaming big enough. Push yourself. Dare to pursue big dreams, and ignore what others may think of your goals—after all, they're your dreams, not theirs.

Make sure your attitude is right and take massive action. The biggest risk isn't failure; it's staying the same and missing out on your true potential.

Key Takeaways

1. **Risk Is Essential for Growth:** Taking risks is necessary to move from where you are to where you want to be. Without stepping outside your comfort zone, you limit your potential.
2. **Marketing Takes Courage and Creativity:** To make a difference, you have to stand out. Whether it's putting your face on a car or trying unconventional strategies, bold moves can amplify your impact.
3. **Build a Team Aligned with Your Vision:** Expanding your team brings new challenges but also new possibilities. Surround yourself with people who are as dedicated to the mission as you are.
4. **Be Willing to Invest in Yourself and Your Dream:** The new office was a big investment, but it showed

commitment to growth. Sometimes, the biggest leaps forward come from putting it all on the line.

5. **Failure Is a Learning Opportunity:** Don't fear failure—embrace it as part of the journey. If you're not experiencing setbacks, your goals might be too small.
6. **Don't Let Others Define Your Path:** People will doubt, question, and critique your choices. Focus on your vision and don't let outside opinions deter you.

Prompt for Reflection

What is one risk you've been avoiding? How might it propel you closer to your dreams if you embraced it?

Final Thought

The biggest risk in life is doing nothing at all. Embrace challenges, take bold steps, and remember: every risk you take brings you one step closer to realizing your dreams.

Chapter 3

Habits & Mindset

"Live every day like it's your last, because someday you're going to be right."

Muhammad Ali

Last year, my daughter Lola had a big wish: she wanted to see the Mall of America. Between her dance and basketball schedules, finding a free weekend was a challenge. But we finally managed to carve out time—a Friday after school to drive up, all day Saturday at the mall, and then a long drive back Sunday so they'd be ready for school on Monday.

To be honest, we weren't sure how the kids would react to such a packed schedule and a long drive. But to our surprise and delight, they were thrilled. Instead of focusing on the long hours on the road, they looked forward to the time we'd all have together. They didn't complain about the quick trip; instead, they saw the adventure ahead. We were proud to see them focusing on the positives, a mindset we actively encourage in our family.

Choosing Positivity Daily

I'm a glass-half-full kind of guy, and I've developed a habit of "filling my cup" every day. My positive mindset didn't come naturally; it was something I cultivated through habit and resilience. Like everyone, I've faced my share of hardships, but choosing to focus on the good has helped me move forward.

Your mindset can shape your entire life. I believe that a positive outlook—or the lack of it—can make or break you. Rewiring your brain to see the positives, especially if you've faced hardship, is no easy task. I recognize that everyone's journey is unique, and there's no one-size-fits-all path to achieving a positive mindset. However, I'd like to share the habits and practices that have helped me stay grounded and resilient, especially during difficult times.

Building Habits Through Life's Changes

My habits have evolved significantly since I started my career with the insurance company in 2005. The arrival of my children, Lola and Hudson, brought the most profound changes. When Lola was born, I knew I needed to be more disciplined with my routine to balance family time with my responsibilities. As my family grew and my business expanded, my daily habits became essential for "winning the day."

In this chapter, I'll walk you through how life's changes—both personal and professional—helped shape the daily habits that support my positive mindset. At the end of the chapter, I'll share practical tips to help you establish and maintain a positive outlook in your own life.

Life's Turning Point: Welcoming Lola

The arrival of my daughter, Lola, in 2012 was a pivotal moment for me. I found out we were expecting while my new office was under construction. I was eagerly awaiting both the completion of the office and Lola's arrival. Then, on February 21st, 2012, Lola entered the world unexpectedly early and was immediately airlifted to a children's hospital, where she stayed for five weeks.

Those five weeks were an emotional rollercoaster. I spent every day at the hospital, praying for her lungs to strengthen. Nothing else mattered; everything else took a back seat. I am forever grateful that Lola grew stronger and was eventually able to come home. Her homecoming marked a new normal for me—a life where family took precedence over everything else.

A Shift in Priorities and Habits

With Lola at home, I knew I needed to make changes at the office to be present in her life. Before Lola's birth, my habits revolved around running daily operations, working long hours, and focusing entirely on building the business. I was in a constant state of hustle, doing whatever it took, whenever it was needed. Early mornings and late nights were the norm, and I rarely took time away from the office.

When Lola arrived, I knew my approach to work had to change. I began to assess how I was spending my time and looked for areas where I could be more efficient. I realized that a lot of my time was tied up in daily tasks I'd carried over from when I was a team member, tasks that were no longer the best use of my time. Shifting my mindset from that of a team member to that of a leader was essential.

One of the most effective strategies I developed was the principle of "do it, delegate it, or delete it." This simple approach became key to my productivity. I receive hundreds of emails daily, so I started time-blocking specific moments each day to respond. Before this, I had a habit of responding to every email as soon as it came in, disrupting my focus and pulling me away from bigger goals. By setting aside time for emails, I could step back, focus on my vision, and avoid being reactive all day.

"Do it, delegate it, or delete it" is as straightforward as it sounds. When I tackle emails, I either take action, delegate the task to someone on my team, or delete it if it doesn't need attention. This approach has allowed me to free up time to focus on growth, leadership, and refining processes.

Embracing Delegation and Leadership

As my skills in delegation improved, I noticed a significant shift in my time. I could now spend more of it on leading and training my team rather than getting bogged down in daily tasks. This has allowed me to step out of the grind and focus on my role as a leader. Of course, I occasionally fall back into old habits, but when that happens, I remind myself to reorient, step back, and refocus on leading.

Time is valuable to me, and I'm committed to creating a life where I can be an effective leader while also being present as a father. My children grow up quickly, and I want to be there for every moment. I'm intentional about crafting a healthy work-life balance that allows me to pursue success and wealth for my family while also enjoying time with them. To do this, I stay disciplined with my routine and take consistent action toward my goals.

"Do It, Delegate It, or Delete It" in Action

In 2014, this approach became even more crucial when my son Hudson was born on August 14th. Adding a newborn to the family made my time management skills all the more essential! With Hudson's arrival, I continued to refine my routine to maximize my time, leading me to discover the power of a solid morning routine.

My morning routine has been pivotal in helping me achieve the balance I want. It allows me to start each day on the right foot, setting the tone for the day ahead. While everyone's routine will look different, here's what works for me.

Crafting My Morning Routine

Each morning, I wake up as soon as my alarm goes off—no snoozing, no bargaining for "five more minutes." I find that starting the day on time is essential to following through on the rest of my morning routine. The first thing I do is wish a happy birthday to all of my Facebook friends. With 5,000 friends, this takes about 20–30 minutes! I also use this time to post positive content on my page, usually around 15-20 posts per day.

Once I'm done with social media, I get dressed, hydrate, and prepare for my workout. A bit of cardio in the morning, accompanied by motivational and educational podcasts, gets both my body and mind moving. I read 10 pages a day, it is a nonnegotiable habit that I have implemented in my daily routine. Feeding my mind with uplifting content first thing in the morning strengthens my mindset and sets me up for a positive day. I'm constantly looking for ways to elevate my office, and listening to experienced leaders and industry experts helps me find new insights to apply to both work and life.

Encouraging a Positive Mindset in My Family

Outside of work, I encourage my children, my girlfriend, and her son to adopt a positive mindset. Each morning on the way to school, I ask the kids to share something they're grateful for. This simple habit helps them start their day with appreciation, focusing on the good in their lives. It's become a cherished routine, and they look forward to sharing what they're grateful for.

I remember a recent family dinner when we went around the table, each of us sharing one thing we were thankful for. When it was Hudson's turn, he said he was grateful for his health. It was a beautiful moment of reflection and a reminder of the importance of gratitude.

We recently had a friend's 14-year-old grandson who was badly injured in an accident. As I write this, he's in his eighth week at the hospital, fighting to recover from a traumatic brain injury. Over the past few weeks, Kelsey and I have shared his journey with our kids, getting emotional as we updated them on his progress. One night, as we sat around the table, Hudson reflected on what this young boy was going through. He shared that he was grateful for his own health, recognizing just how precious it is. That moment hit us hard. It's incredible to watch your children stop, think, and express gratitude in such a genuine way. This kind of gratitude exercise has become a powerful part of our family routine, something we all place immense value on.

Practicing, listening, and embracing positivity has profoundly impacted my life—both personally and professionally. It's also had a ripple effect on the people around me. At the end of the day, life is short. Why walk through it with a negative mindset? A key lesson I've learned about cultivating positivity is to be intentional about where you focus your emotional energy.

Surround Yourself with the Right People

Pay close attention to the people around you. If you're working on nurturing a positive outlook, step away from negative environments and individuals who bring you down. Think about it—are there rooms where you leave feeling drained? Rooms filled with people who don't support you? If so, stop stepping into those rooms. Instead, surround yourself with people who lift you up, encourage you, and appreciate you for who you truly are. In the end, those who truly matter will be there through both triumphs and setbacks. Take comfort in knowing you have constants in life—people who allow you to be vulnerable and who support your growth.

Personally, I seek out rooms full of people who share a positive mindset and support each other's growth. That's why I make it a priority to be involved in masterminds and study groups. In these spaces, I connect with other agents, sharing what's working, what isn't, and learning from each other's experiences. One thing I've realized: learning from others' success is immensely powerful. If someone else has reached a goal, why can't you? Aligning your mindset with successful people can change your life.

Seek Solutions, Not Problems

Another thing I've noticed about the people in these groups—they are solution-oriented, not problem-oriented. No matter the obstacle, they focus on finding a way through it rather than making excuses. Spend time with people who see the good in life, and you'll notice a shift in your own mindset.

I've found that many positive people have faced immense challenges, but they don't dwell on the negatives. They look at difficulties from a different perspective, turning obstacles into opportunities. For myself and others who attend masterminds, there's no finish line; it's the journey itself that brings happiness. People who lack a sense of purpose or the desire for growth are often the ones who feel unfulfilled. There's so much joy in setting goals, seeing progress, and taking on new challenges.

Continuously Grow and Set Goals

A consistent trait among people with a growth mindset is their drive to constantly improve. They wake up each day aiming to be better than they were yesterday. Happiness, after all, comes from within. It's something you build every day through intentional actions.

Goal-setting is another practice that keeps my mindset positive. Whether it's planning a family trip or a professional milestone, I set dates and create things to look forward to. For instance, Kelsey my girlfriend and I are surprising the kids with a trip to Miami right after Christmas. We're already imagining their reactions—Gio running in circles, Lola exclaiming "What?!" and Hudson jumping on the couch, shouting, "Let's go!" We decided to do fewer material gifts this year and instead focus on creating memories. This trip has been in the works for months, and the anticipation has been almost as fun as the trip itself will be. Setting goals like this keeps us excited and focused on creating experiences that bring joy.

Goal-Setting in Business

Goal-setting is equally powerful in my professional life. When I first became an agent, I noticed a photo of a beautiful vacation in one of the executives' offices. When I asked about it, he explained it was from a trip for the company's top agents. Back then, I didn't believe I'd ever make it to that level. But I did. How? Through mindset and consistent habits. Every January 1, I reset my goals to zero and strive to qualify for that year's trip. This year's destination was Bora-Bora, and I set the goal right away to make it. By March, the office had already qualified for the year. It's about impact—the more people we help, the more goals we meet.

In summary, my habits and mindset are the foundation for everything I've achieved. The way I begin each day, the gratitude I cultivate, the goals I set—these elements work together to keep my mind moving forward and my outlook positive.

Goal-setting in this way doesn't just give me something to look forward to; it also drives our impact. Setting clear goals—big and small—keeps my habits in check and my outlook positive. So far, I've shared some life changes that taught me the importance of delegation, building my morning routine, and goal-setting for personal and professional growth.

A Positive Mindset in Action

One habit that's transformed my work environment is starting every client meeting with a simple question: "What's going good today?" Now, I'll ask you the same: What's going well for you today? Is it your health? Family? Relationships? Take a moment each day to reflect on something you're grateful for.

This question reframes the day, shifting the focus to positivity. It's also changed my approach to challenges. Before working on my mindset, I had more of a team member mentality, focusing heavily on daily reports and sometimes beginning the day with negative energy. Now, with a CEO mindset, I go into each day with high energy and a problem-solving focus. I know that challenges can be turned into opportunities with the right perspective.

Whatever you do, challenges will always arise. But when you shift your mindset to view the bigger picture, those same challenges become chances to grow. In situations that don't go as planned, I ask myself, "Is this controllable?" If it's not, I let it go. If it is, I handle it to the best of my ability and find peace in the effort. Each day is a fresh start, an opportunity to keep building a legacy, whether that means striving for a healthier work-life balance, financial freedom, or personal fulfillment.

It's never too late to give your mindset a makeover. Creating a positive mindset takes hard work and daily dedication. When you start to see how it impacts every area of your life, you'll wonder why you didn't start sooner.

Key Takeaways

1. **Prioritize Positivity**: A positive mindset doesn't come by chance; it's a choice you make every day. Embrace each morning as an opportunity to approach the day with a focus on gratitude, growth, and optimism.

2. **Surround Yourself with Uplifting People**: The people around you affect your mindset more than you may realize. Spend time with those who support you, inspire growth, and bring out the best in you.
3. **Define and Revisit Your Goals**: Big goals can transform your mindset and habits. Keep them visible, set dates, and take consistent action toward them. Remember, a clear vision gives your daily routines direction and purpose.
4. **Practice Gratitude Daily**: Asking yourself, "What's going good today?" encourages a positive start to the day. Gratitude is a powerful tool for resetting your mindset, building resilience, and reinforcing your goals.
5. **Turn Challenges into Opportunities**: Life will bring obstacles, but with the right mindset, each challenge can become a stepping stone toward growth. Train yourself to ask, "Is this controllable?" and focus your energy on constructive actions.
6. **Embrace a "Do It, Delegate It, or Delete It" Mentality**: Effective time management fuels positivity. By learning to delegate and time-block, you free yourself from constant reactivity, allowing for clearer focus on your larger goals

Prompt for Reflection

What is one small but powerful habit you can incorporate into your day to build a more positive mindset? Are there any people, routines, or environments that might be holding you back from your goals?

Final Thought

Remember, a positive mindset is not just about avoiding negativity but about intentionally creating a life you want to live. Every day offers the chance to shape your habits, define your goals, and grow closer to the person you're working to become.

Chapter 4

Mind Over Matter

"Whether you think you can, or you think you can't – you're right."

Henry Ford

A positive mindset is more than just a catchphrase you hear tossed around in motivational speeches; it's a powerful tool that can shape your life and influence the world around you. I've learned that, just like a muscle, your mind needs constant training to stay strong and resilient. I've been through my share of valleys, and it's there, not on the peaks, where I've learned the most.

Building a Positive Framework

My positive mindset was nurtured early on, thanks to my parents. I can still hear my dad's voice, reminding me: "Can't" never did anything." Whether it was on the ball field or in the classroom, the word "can't" was simply not allowed in our house. This early reinforcement shaped my approach to life, both professionally and personally. Every day is a new opportunity – that's something I carry with me into the office and into my life. I have a motto: *Just getting started.* It's more than words; it's a reminder that no matter where I am or what I've achieved, there's always room for growth.

Positivity is Contagious

One thing I've learned about a positive mindset is that it's contagious. The energy you bring to the room influences everyone around you, whether that's your team, your family, or even strangers. Unfortunately, the same is true for negativity. So, you've got to be intentional about feeding positivity into your daily life. It's not just about thinking happy thoughts; it's about what you consume mentally, the habits you create, and how you set up your day to win.

So, how do you maintain that level of positivity? It starts with intentionality. From the moment you open your eyes in the morning, you have to be mindful of what you feed your mind. For me, it's about starting the day with gratitude and feeding my mind with things that lift me up, like positive content, exercise, and surrounding myself with the right people.

The Power of Self-Talk

A positive mindset isn't just about outward actions—it starts inside with how you talk to yourself. Confidence is key, but it's something you have to build over time, not something you're born with. Self-confidence takes practice. It's a matter of repeating the same actions, trying and failing, but never losing momentum.

Positive self-talk plays a crucial role here. What you say to yourself is more important than what you say to others because it lays the foundation for your mindset. If your internal dialogue is filled with negativity, your external actions will reflect that. On the flip side, when you intentionally practice positive self-talk, it builds resilience, confidence, and a belief in yourself that can't be easily shaken.

Who's in Your Circle?

My parents always told me, "You become who you hang around," and I've found this to be one of life's greatest truths. Look at the people around you—are they lifting you up or pulling you down? There's a concept I call the "crab mindset." Imagine crabs in a net; one almost makes it out, but the others pull it back down. The same happens with people in your life if you're not careful. Negative people, whether they mean to or not, can keep you from reaching your full potential.

That's why it's so important to do a regular inventory of your circle. If someone in your life is consistently bringing negativity, you may need to set boundaries or even distance yourself to protect your mindset. On the other hand, if you've got people who inspire and uplift you, draw closer to them. Their positivity will rub off on you. The Law of Attraction, is not just an idea, it is a Law.

Physical Movement Fuels Mental Strength

One non-negotiable in my life is daily exercise. I make it a point to break a sweat every morning because it's scientifically proven to boost your mood and give you positive energy. It's not just about physical health; it's about feeding your mind with positivity and setting the tone for your day. The discipline of a daily workout spills over into every other aspect of my life. The same way you build your body's strength, you build your mental resilience.

Focus on What You Can Control

In life, there are two types of situations: the ones you can control and the ones you can't. One of the most crucial lessons I've learned is to let go of the uncontrollable and pour my energy into the things I can change. If you focus on things outside of your control, it starts to own you. It owns your thoughts, your actions, and ultimately your outcomes. The key to staying positive is to take massive action on what's in your hands and let the rest go.

The Valleys Teach You More Than the Peaks

As much as we'd like life to be smooth sailing, the truth is that our greatest growth often comes from the toughest moments. I've learned more in the valleys than I ever did on the peaks. It's when you're down and out that you find out what you're made of. Challenges give you the opportunity to tap into resources you didn't know you had, whether that's reaching out for help, leaning on others, or simply finding the resilience to keep going.

I've been through personal and professional hardships that could've knocked me out of the game, but instead, I chose to view those moments as opportunities to grow. And that's what you have to remember when you hit a low point: it's not the end; it's a chance to rebuild stronger than before.

Intentional Living Drives Success

Success isn't something that happens by accident; it's the result of intentional actions taken consistently over time. Whether it's my son Hudson working with his private basketball trainer or my daughter Lola honing her skills on the volleyball court, their success doesn't come from luck. It comes from hours of practice, discipline, and intentional effort. The same goes for you. Are you living life by chance or by choice? Are your actions aligned with your goals, or are you just hoping things will magically work out? The truth is, nothing worth having comes easy. If you want a positive mindset, a successful career, or strong relationships, it all requires intentional effort every single day.

Key Takeaways

1. **Positive Mindset is Intentional:** Positivity doesn't happen by accident; it requires intentional action. Start your day by feeding your mind with positive content, whether that's through exercise, self-talk, or surrounding yourself with the right people.
2. **Self-Talk Shapes Your Reality:** The way you speak to yourself is crucial. Practice positive self-talk, especially

during difficult moments. Your inner dialogue sets the tone for your actions and your outlook on life.

3. **Evaluate Your Circle:** Who you surround yourself with matters. Regularly assess whether the people in your life lift you up or pull you down. Don't bc afraid to set boundaries to protect your mindset.
4. **Focus on What You Can Control:** Let go of what you can't control and channel your energy into what you can. Taking action on the controllables will keep you moving forward in a positive direction.
5. **Growth Happens in the Valleys:** The most valuable lessons often come from the hardest times. Don't fear the valleys; embrace them as opportunities to grow stronger.
6. **Intentional Actions Drive Results:** Success, in any area of life, comes from consistent, intentional actions. Whether it's improving your mindset, career, or relationships, it all starts with being deliberate about your choices.

Prompt for Reflection

Are your daily habits aligned with the life you want to live? What is one small action you can take starting today to move closer to your goals, both personally and professionally?

Final Thought

Remember, the only limits you have are the ones you place on yourself. Start each day with a mindset of opportunity, embrace the challenges, and keep pushing forward. The journey won't always be easy, but it will be worth it. Keep going—you're just getting started.

Part 2

The Outside Game

Chapter 5

The Opinions of Others

Letting Go and Moving Forward

"What other people think of you is none of your business."

Anonymous

Early in my career, I made the mistake of caring far too much about what others thought of me. I was a people pleaser, driven by the opinions of those around me. Every piece of feedback, every canceled policy, every sideways glance felt personal. It wasn't just about business; it was about my self-worth, and I carried that weight far longer than I should have. Over time, though, I realized that constantly chasing validation from others only held me back. This chapter is all about letting go of the need for approval, developing thick skin, and focusing on what truly matters—your growth and your goals.

People Pleasing: A Trap for Your Growth

When I first became an agent, I thought success meant keeping everyone happy. If someone canceled their insurance, I'd take it personally. If someone had a negative opinion about me or my business, it felt like an attack on my character. I believed that to grow my business, I needed to please everyone. But that mindset turned out to be one of the biggest mistakes I made early on.

Today, I'd laugh it off and go about my day. But back then, the opinions of others weighed heavily on me.

Even worse, I let the opinions of total strangers affect my confidence. A gas station attendant once told me that my business wouldn't survive because everyone in town was already loyal to a competitor. It hurt to hear, and instead of brushing it off, I internalized it. Those moments are prime examples of how giving too much weight to the opinions of others can derail your mindset and your confidence.

Learning to Tune Out the Noise

One of the most important lessons I've learned is that opinions are just noise. Not every opinion matters. My dad used to tell me, "The higher you climb, the more people will try to pull you down." He was right. The more successful you become, the more opinions you'll encounter. Some will be positive, but many will be rooted in jealousy, insecurity, or simply misunderstanding.

When I wrapped my first vehicle with my business logo and image back in 2010, it caused a stir in my small town. People criticized me, called it arrogant, and spread gossip on social media. For years, that feedback bothered me. I took every comment to heart, wondering if I was doing something wrong. But over time, I realized that those opinions had nothing to do with me and everything to do with how others perceived my success. Today, I've had my vehicles wrapped for over a decade, and some of the same people who criticized me are now asking for advice on marketing. Funny how that works.

The key is to develop tough skin and block out the noise. Focus on the opinions of those who inspire you, those who have been where you want to go. As my dad said, the more you build, the more opinions will come out of the woodwork. You can't let them get in your way.

Authenticity is Your Greatest Tool

To truly succeed, you have to be yourself. Authenticity is your strongest tool, and it's the antidote to caring about what others think. The more genuine you are, the less their opinions will matter. When you're focused on pleasing everyone else, you lose sight of who you are and what you want. But when you look inward—when you focus on the person in the mirror rather than the voices outside the window—you unlock your potential.

There's freedom in authenticity. When you stop worrying about what others think, you start living for yourself, making decisions that align with your values and your goals. You'll never please everyone, and that's okay. Trying to do so only leads to burnout and frustration.

Focus on What You Can Control

The truth is, you have no control over someone else's opinion of you. No matter how hard you try, you can't change how others perceive you. But what you can control is your response. Are you going to let their opinions dictate your decisions, or are you going to focus on what truly matters—your goals, your dreams, and your loved ones?

One of the best pieces of advice I can give is to stop chasing validation. Whether it's social media likes, approval from peers, or recognition from strangers, none of it truly matters in the grand scheme of things. Instead, focus on the controllables—your work, your family, your health. When you narrow your focus on what's within your control, you free yourself from the weight of others' opinions.

Resilience – The Key to Blocking Out the Noise

Developing resilience is crucial if you want to grow. When you stop caring about what everyone thinks, you unlock a sense of freedom that's hard to describe. Suddenly, the opinions that once weighed you down no longer have any power. You're no longer controlled by the expectations of others, and you can live your life with more clarity and purpose.

Letting go of people-pleasing reduces stress and anxiety. It also gives you more energy to focus on what truly matters—your goals, your relationships, and your well-being. Imagine how much lighter you'll feel when you stop tying your self-worth to what others think. The relief that comes from releasing that burden is life-changing.

The Right People Will Find You

One of the most powerful realizations I've had is that when you stop trying to be someone you're not, the right people will naturally come into your life. When you stop pretending and start living authentically, you attract those who truly align with your values and goals. And the best part? You no longer waste energy on trying to impress the wrong people.

I've learned that trying to please everyone only erodes your self-esteem and self-worth. It's exhausting, and it never leads to happiness. Once you embrace who you are and stop seeking external validation, you'll build stronger, more meaningful relationships with those who genuinely care about you.

The Freedom of Letting Go

The freedom that comes from letting go of other people's opinions is like nothing else. When you stop caring about the opinions of others, you become more focused, more productive, and more at peace with yourself. You're no longer weighed down by anxiety or self-doubt, and you start making decisions that are aligned with your own values.

Social media is one of the biggest traps for those who care too much about what others think. It's easy to fall into the cycle of seeking likes, comments, and validation online. But once you let go of the need for approval, you can use social media as a tool for connection and creativity, rather than a source of stress.

Key Takeaways

1. **Not Everyone's Opinion Matters:** It's important to filter out the noise. Focus on the opinions of those who inspire you and have been where you want to go, rather than those who criticize from a place of insecurity or jealousy.
2. **Authenticity is Key:** Being true to yourself will help you let go of the need for approval. When you live authentically, the opinions of others will have less power over you.
3. **Focus on the Controllables:** You can't control how others see you, but you can control your response. Focus on what you can change—your goals, your relationships, and your personal growth.
4. **Build Resilience:** The more you build your resilience, the less you'll care about external opinions. Developing a thick skin frees you from the anxiety and stress of people-pleasing.
5. **The Right People Will Find You:** When you stop pretending and start being yourself, you'll attract the right people into your life—those who support and align with your values.

Prompt for Reflection

How much energy are you spending on worrying about what others think? What steps can you take to focus more on yourself and your goals rather than seeking external validation?

Final Thought

You can't control what others think, but you can control how much you let it affect you. Focus on being true to yourself, and let the opinions of others fade into the background. The freedom you'll gain from letting go is worth more than the validation of strangers

Chapter 6

Processes and Consistency

The Framework for Success

"Success doesn't happen by accident; it's built on a foundation of consistent processes."

Anonymous

In any business, team, or organization, processes and consistency are the backbone of success. It's the structure that allows goals to be met, standards to be upheld, and growth to happen. As a business owner, I've come to see that having key processes in place—and sticking to them—is what sets high-performing teams apart. In this chapter, we'll dive into the essential processes that drive my business, the value of consistency, and how daily actions can make all the difference.

The Power of Daily Communication

One of the biggest keys to our team's success is daily communication. Not weekly, not monthly—daily. Every morning from 8:30 to 9:00, we meet to go over urgent items, calendar priorities, and any pressing issues. I picked up this habit from Larry Burton, an agent from Chester, Illinois, whose team met every single day. Those 30 minutes lay the foundation for our day, allowing us to align on priorities and stay focused.

Our meetings have structure that varies by day, keeping things both organized and engaging. For example:

- **Monday** is for reviewing the past week's results and setting improvement goals. I also take this time to share a sales process or strategy.
- **Tuesday** is "Positive Tuesday," where each team member shares something positive from their business or personal life. This intentional focus on positivity helps us reset after a busy Monday and sets a strong tone for the week.

- **Wednesday** is about big-picture goals, where we look at our yearly metrics and evaluate where we stand on annual targets.
- **Thursday** is all about role-playing. We practice different scenarios, from product conversations to handling objections, so everyone is prepared and improving.
- **Friday** is dedicated to product knowledge. We dive into the features, benefits, and marketing of a product to ensure everyone is fully educated.

Daily meetings are more than just a routine; they're an investment in our team's communication, morale, and alignment. This consistency has allowed us to stay adaptable and productive, no matter what challenges arise.

One-on-One Meetings: A Personalized Approach to Growth

As a leader, part of my role is to provide individualized support to my team. Depending on each team member's role and experience, I hold one-on-one meetings either weekly or monthly. These sessions are focused on their personal growth, goals, and challenges. My favorite way to start these meetings is by asking, "What's on your mind?" It's a simple question, but it opens the door for honest conversation.

In these meetings, we review their numbers, activity levels, and skillsets, and I look for ways to help them progress. My role is to offer guidance and support, but ultimately, it's up to them to execute. As the saying goes, "You can lead a horse to water, but you can't make it drink." By holding these one-on-ones, I'm able to foster growth and accountability, helping each team member reach their full potential.

Annual Planning Meetings – Setting the Vision

Each year, our team gets together for an annual planning meeting where we review our goals, refine our processes, and set the vision for the year ahead. It's an opportunity for us to break from routine, step back, and take a big-picture look at where we're going. We also make a point to enjoy ourselves, often holding this meeting on a weekend or during a team outing. This isn't just about planning; it's about building relationships and fostering trust within our team. When we understand each other on a personal level, our work culture strengthens, making it easier to reach our shared goals.

Standards and Agreements – The Foundation of Accountability

In my early days, I focused on setting expectations for my team. But I've since learned that expectations without agreement can lead to miscommunication. Now, I focus on creating "standards and agreements." By involving the team in conversations about what's expected, we create agreements that everyone buys into. This shared understanding fosters accountability, ensuring that each team member knows what's required and is willing to commit to it.

Setting standards doesn't mean everyone gets it right 100% of the time, but it does provide a clear benchmark. It's a guide for how we operate and hold each other accountable. As John Maxwell says, "Everything rises and falls on leadership," and I believe that's equally true for standards.

The CRM System: Follow-Up as a Key Process

Consistency in follow-up is one of the most underrated skills in business. To make this process seamless, we rely on a CRM system. I always say, "Buy or die," meaning we follow up persistently until we've either made a sale or definitively closed the door. Studies show that it often takes five to seven touches to convert a lead, but many people give up after just one or two. The CRM system ensures that follow-ups don't fall through the cracks and helps us build long-term relationships, even with people who haven't yet bought from us.

This tool allows us to stay organized and maintain persistence. If we're not following up consistently, we're losing opportunities. By tracking our interactions and setting reminders, we make sure no one slips through the cracks, ultimately driving higher conversion rates and stronger relationships.

Urgency and Speed – The Winning Formula

One of the most significant factors in success is a sense of urgency. Speed matters in today's fast-paced world. Clients expect quick responses, and if you delay, you risk losing their interest. I have a rule: if something takes less than two minutes to complete, do it immediately. This practice has dramatically boosted our team's productivity and responsiveness.

Those who work with urgency generally see better results. When a client contacts us, a quick response shows we value their time and business. It's the Amazon effect—clients expect instant service, and we aim to deliver it. When team members understand the importance of speed and urgency, they're more likely to take immediate action, which has a direct impact on our results.

Organization – Inbox and Calendar Management

A well-organized inbox and calendar are essential for productivity. I've learned this firsthand, and I stress it to my team. When I meet with new team members, one of the first things I look at is their inbox. If it's cluttered with hundreds of unread emails, I know they're struggling with organization. I coach them to process each email with three options: do it, delegate it, or delete it.

The same goes for calendar management. A blank calendar means you're not planning effectively. I encourage everyone to block out time for important tasks, such as power hours for focused work. By setting aside dedicated time, they can concentrate on high-impact activities without constant distractions.

Discipline and Power Hours

Discipline is a skill that only improves with experience. One of the tools we use to build this is "power hours." During these time blocks, we focus exclusively on one specific task with a clear goal in mind. Whether it's client follow-ups, outreach, or paperwork, power hours drive focus and eliminate distractions. Discipline is key to making these sessions effective. It's not easy, especially at first, but the more you commit to it, the more productive you'll become.

Keeping Score – Daily Metrics

If you're not keeping score, you're missing out on valuable insights. Tracking metrics daily allows us to stay on top of our goals and measure progress. For my team, we play a game inspired by baseball: a single line of business is a single, two lines are a double, three lines are a triple, and four lines are a home run. At the end of the week, if we hit our targets, the team receives a reward.

Keeping score creates focus and brings out everyone's competitive spirit. It's amazing how engaged the team becomes when there's a scoreboard involved. It turns ordinary tasks into something fun and motivating, and it keeps everyone focused on contributing to our overall goals.

Transparency and Accountability

Transparency is a critical part of our culture. By being open about numbers, goals, and performance, I build trust within the team. When everyone understands where we stand and what's at stake, it drives accountability. There's no room for assumptions; we're all on the same page. Processes and systems are non-negotiable, but it's transparency that helps our team feel like part of a bigger mission. Accountability becomes natural when you're invested in the outcome and clear on expectations.

Attitude, Ability, Action – The Formula for Success

In our meetings, I emphasize one formula: Attitude + Ability + Action - Excuses = Success. When I see a gap in someone's performance, it usually falls within one of these categories. We work together to identify which part needs improvement and develop a plan to address it. A positive attitude, skill development, and consistent action are the core ingredients of success. Remove the excuses, and you're left with results.

Key Takeaways

1. **Consistency is Key:** Success in any business is built on consistent processes. Daily communication, scheduled meetings, and clear standards keep the team aligned and productive.
2. **Communication is Foundational:** Daily meetings keep everyone on the same page, while one-on-ones and planning sessions offer personalized growth

opportunities. Effective communication creates trust and fosters a stronger team dynamic.

3. **Standards and Agreements Over Expectations:** When team standards are agreed upon rather than imposed, accountability naturally follows. A team that understands and agrees on standards is more likely to uphold them.
4. **Urgency Drives Results:** In today's world, quick action is essential. A sense of urgency not only improves client satisfaction but also boosts team productivity.
5. **Organization and Planning Build Efficiency:** Structured inboxes, well-managed calendars, and planned power hours help streamline work, reduce overwhelm, and increase focus.
6. **Track Progress Daily:** Keeping score on a daily basis maintains motivation, encourages healthy competition, and provides valuable insights for improvement.
7. **Transparency Builds Trust:** When goals and performance are shared openly, accountability follows. A transparent culture fosters investment in the team's shared mission.
8. **Attitude, Ability, Action – The Path to Success:** Success is driven by a positive attitude, continuous skill development, and consistent action. Eliminating excuses makes space for growth and results.

Prompt for Reflection

Which daily processes could you implement to boost consistency in your work? How can you create a culture of urgency, organization, and accountability within your team?

Final Thought

Success is no accident; it's the result of discipline, consistency, and focus. When you commit to the right processes, you set yourself up for growth, resilience, and lasting achievement. Stay committed to your daily actions—they're the foundation of your future success.

Chapter 7

Massive Action

The Key to Overcoming Fear

"You miss 100% of the shots you don't take."

Wayne Gretzky

Taking action is the bridge between where you are and where you want to be. It's easy to talk about goals and dreams, but nothing changes until you make a move. Throughout my life, I've seen firsthand how massive action—deliberate, consistent steps—can create momentum, overcome fear, and drive success. This chapter explores the power of action, the barriers that hold people back, and how to build the habits that keep you moving forward.

Taking the First Step: Overcoming Fear

In my early years, fear often held me back. Whether it was making that first sales call or trying something new in my business, I'd hesitate. My mind would play out the worst-case scenarios—what if they said no? What if I failed? But the truth is, you'll never know unless you try. My dad and my coaches always told me, "If you don't swing the bat, you can't hit the ball." It's a lesson I took to heart, both in baseball and in life.

Fear of failure is one of the biggest reasons people hold back from taking action. But what I've learned is that failure isn't the opposite of success—it's a part of it. Every time you swing and miss, you're learning, adapting, and getting better. That's why I've always encouraged my team to get comfortable being uncomfortable. It's in those uncomfortable moments that growth happens.

The Role of Belief in Action

Belief is a crucial component of taking action. If you don't believe in what you're doing, you'll never be able to take the massive action required for success. I've seen this time and again with my team members—those who believe in the value they're offering are the ones who take the most action.

They don't see themselves as selling; they see themselves as providing value and providing education.

Building belief takes time and experience. When you practice daily, your confidence grows, and your belief in what you're doing deepens. This belief fuels your willingness to take action, even when it's difficult. It helps you see that you're not imposing on others; you're offering something of value.

Focus and Time Blocking: Creating Space for Action

Even with strong belief, taking action can be challenging without focus. Distractions are everywhere—our phones, social media, everyday responsibilities. To counter this, I use a strategy called time blocking. Time blocking means setting aside specific periods for focused, uninterrupted work. It's about being intentional with your time.

For example, if I need to make client calls, I'll block out an hour just for that. No emails, no social media, just focused action. This practice has transformed my productivity and has allowed me to consistently take massive action. It's not about working more hours—it's about making the hours you work count.

Small Goals, Big Progress

People often get overwhelmed by the idea of taking massive action because they think it means doing something huge all at once. But in reality, it's about breaking big goals down into small, manageable steps. How do you eat an elephant? One bite at a time.

When you set smaller goals, you create opportunities for quick wins, which build momentum. These wins give you the motivation to keep going, even when the bigger goal still feels far off. Consistency is more important than intensity. It's better to do a little bit each day than to burn out trying to do everything at once.

The Importance of Daily Practice

Whether you're building a business, learning a new skill, or trying to improve yourself, daily practice is the key to progress. I often tell my kids, Hudson and Lola, that you can't expect to get better at basketball or volleyball if you only practice once a week. It's the same in life—consistent, daily action compounds over time.

I've made it a point to practice daily habits that support my growth, like reading 10 pages of a book every day for the rest of my life. It doesn't matter if I'm tired or not feeling up to it; I've committed to it, and that consistency makes all the difference. It's a small action, but it has a big impact over time. The same goes for other habits—whether it's making calls, following up with clients, or learning something new.

Failure is a Setup, Not a Setback

One of the most important lessons I've learned is that failure is not a setback; it's a setup for growth. When I coach my team, I look at their activity levels and ask, "Are you failing enough to win?" It might sound counterintuitive, but the more you fail, the closer you get to success. Each failure is an opportunity to learn, adapt, and improve.

I've seen people overthink their actions, trying to predict every outcome before they even make a move. But the truth is, you can't predict how things will turn out until you try. The only way to get better is to take action, fail, and adjust. Don't let fear of failure hold you back—embrace it as a necessary part of your journey.

Procrastination: The Enemy of Action

Procrastination is one of the biggest obstacles to taking action. It's easy to put things off, especially when they're difficult or uncomfortable. But procrastination only delays progress. The longer you wait, the harder it becomes to get started.

To beat procrastination, you have to push yourself to do the things you don't feel like doing. It's not about waiting for the perfect moment; it's about taking action even when it's tough. I've found that when you start with one small step, it becomes easier to keep going. The hardest part is often just getting started.

Learning from the Best

Surrounding yourself with people who inspire you is one of the best ways to keep taking action

If you want to grow, find people who have already achieved what you're aiming for. Learn from them, study their habits, and apply those lessons to your own life. Success leaves clues, and the more you can learn from others, the faster you'll reach your own goals.

Progress Over Perfection

A lot of people get stuck because they're waiting for the perfect moment or the perfect plan before they take action. But perfection is an illusion—it doesn't exist. If you're waiting for everything to be just right, you'll never get started. It's better to focus on progress, not perfection.

Every step you take, no matter how small, is a step closer to your goal. I always remind myself that pressure is a privilege. The opportunity to take action, to feel that sense of urgency, is something to be grateful for. It means you're moving forward, and that's what matters most.

The Power of Consistent Learning

Taking action isn't just about doing—it's also about learning. I believe in the mantra *always be learning* (ABL). Every day is an opportunity to grow, whether it's through reading, listening to podcasts, or engaging with others in your field. But knowledge alone isn't enough—you have to put that knowledge into practice.

It's like having a library card but never checking out a book. Or going to a gas station without pumping gas. You have to apply what you've learned if you want to see results. Action turns knowledge into growth, and growth leads to success.

Sacrifice: What Are You Willing to Give Up?

Taking massive action often requires sacrifice. It might mean giving up time, comfort, or even certain relationships that are holding you back. The question is, what are you willing to sacrifice to achieve your goals? Are you willing to give up the comfort of routine for the discomfort of growth?

Success requires trade-offs. It's about choosing to put your time and energy into the things that matter most. When you're willing to make those sacrifices, you'll find that your progress accelerates.

Key Takeaways

1. **Action Overcomes Fear:** The first step is often the hardest, but taking action is the only way to push past fear. Remember, failure isn't the end; it's a setup for success.
2. **Believe in What You Do:** A strong belief in your goals makes action easier. When you trust in the value of your work, every step feels meaningful.
3. **Focus with Time Blocking:** Set aside dedicated time to work on your most important tasks. Intentional, focused time leads to consistent action and progress.
4. **Small Steps Lead to Big Wins:** Break larger goals into smaller, manageable steps. Consistent, small actions build momentum and keep you moving forward.
5. **Embrace Failure as Part of Success:** Failures are opportunities to learn, adapt, and grow. Don't let fear of failure hold you back—use it as fuel to improve.

6. **Fight Procrastination:** Push yourself to take action, even when it's tough. Starting is often the hardest part, but momentum builds quickly once you begin.
7. **Learn from Those Who Inspire You:** Surround yourself with people who are where you want to be. Success leaves clues—apply what you learn from others.
8. **Progress, Not Perfection:** Waiting for the perfect moment only delays progress. Focus on taking steps forward, and let growth happen over time.

Prompt for Reflection

Are there any areas where fear is holding you back from taking action?
What small actions can you take today to move closer to your goals?

Final Thought

Massive action is the bridge between your dreams and reality. It's not about waiting for the right moment—it's about creating it through consistent effort. Embrace action, embrace growth, and watch your potential unfold.

Chapter 8

The Power of Social Media

"Your brand is what people say about you when you're not in the room."

Jeff Bezos

Social media has become one of the most transformative tools of our time. It's no longer just a way to stay in touch with friends or share vacation photos—it's a platform to build relationships, influence change, and establish trust. For me, social media has evolved from a place of skepticism to one of the most valuable assets in both my personal and professional life.

Looking back, I resisted the idea of diving into social media. My business was thriving with traditional methods, and I didn't see the need to branch out into a space that seemed, at the time, too crowded and impersonal. But one pivotal conversation with my father changed that perspective. His advice to embrace the digital era opened my eyes to the vast potential of connecting authentically with others online.

The Beginning of My Social Media Journey

My father's words stuck with me in the spring of 2010: "Justin, you need to get on social media—it's the future." At the time, I wasn't convinced. I relied on referrals and word-of-mouth marketing, which were working well enough. Social media seemed like an unnecessary distraction.

But as I started to notice the growing role social media played in people's lives, I decided to give it a try. What began as an experiment turned into a foundational piece of my business strategy. Social media wasn't just about marketing—it became a way to connect with people on a deeper level.

Be Genuine

One of the first lessons I learned about social media is that authenticity wins. People don't want to engage with overly polished sales pitches; they want to connect with real people.

That's why my approach has always been to share who I am—my values, hobbies, family life, and the lessons I've learned along the way.

If you follow me online, you'll see that I rarely post directly about my business. Instead, I focus on sharing moments from my life—whether it's fishing with my kids, motivational quotes, or a funny story. People connect with people, not products. When they see the person behind the brand, trust naturally follows.

Building a Digital Presence

Social media isn't just a tool for communication; it's a stage where you get to share your story. For me, it's also a daily reminder of the journey I'm on. Each morning, I spend time wishing my Facebook friends a happy birthday and reflecting on memories from the past 14 years. This practice keeps me grounded and reminds me of how far I've come.

My posting schedule is consistent—I share content 20 to 30 times a day. This level of activity may seem intense, but it's what keeps my audience engaged and my brand top of mind. Whether it's a motivational post, a glimpse into my hobbies, or a family update, every piece of content serves a purpose. I started with a smaller number of posts per day and have steadily increase the amount over time, push yourself to start small and grow the number per day.

Setting the Tone

One of my favorite ways to start the day is by reflecting on what I'm grateful for. This practice doesn't just boost my own mindset—it sets the tone for my interactions on social media. Gratitude is contagious, and I believe it's one of the best ways to build genuine connections.

Each morning, I make it a point to ask myself and my family: "What are you grateful for today?" Sharing this exercise online has inspired others to adopt the practice, creating a ripple effect of positivity.

Connecting with Your Audience

Social media has given me the ability to connect with people I might never have met otherwise. It's a platform to share not just my successes but also my struggles and lessons learned. Over time, these connections have led to meaningful relationships—both personal and professional.

What I've found is that the more authentic you are, the stronger the connections you'll build. By sharing my life openly, I've been able to establish trust with my audience. When people see the real you, they're more likely to reach out when they need help or guidance.

Social Media as a Business Tool

For any business, visibility is key. Social media is like having a digital storefront that's open 24/7. It's where people come to learn about you, your values, and what you stand for. That's why consistency is so important.

Every post I make is intentional. It's about creating value, whether that's through inspiration, education, or entertainment. And while I don't post directly about my business often, the connections I've built online have naturally translated into opportunities.

Navigating Negativity

One of the challenges of social media is dealing with negativity. Whether it's a negative comment or an unproductive debate, it's important to set boundaries. For me, this means curating my online environment to focus on positivity and growth.

If someone consistently brings negativity into my space, I don't hesitate to block them. Social media should be a tool for connection and inspiration, not a source of stress.

Lessons from Study Groups

One of the most impactful ways I've used social media is to connect with like-minded individuals through masterminds and study groups. These communities are filled with people who share a growth mindset and are willing to learn from each other's successes and failures.

What I've learned is that surrounding yourself with solution-oriented people is invaluable. These groups have taught me the importance of collaboration and the power of sharing knowledge.

Creating a Legacy Online

At its core, social media is about storytelling. It's a way to document your journey, share your values, and leave a lasting legacy. For me, it's a digital scrapbook—a place to capture the moments that matter most.

Whether it's a post about my family, a motivational quote, or a lesson I've learned, every piece of content adds to the story I'm building. And while the tools and platforms may change, the purpose remains the same: to connect, inspire, and make a difference.

Conclusion

Social media is more than just a tool—it's an extension of who you are. By showing up authentically, consistently, and with a purpose, you can create meaningful connections and leave a lasting impact.

It's not about chasing likes or followers; it's about building relationships and adding value to the lives of others. When used intentionally, social media can be one of the most powerful tools for achieving your goals and building a legacy.

Takeaways

1. **Authenticity Builds Trust**
   Share the real you—your values, hobbies, and life lessons. People connect with people, not products, and trust grows when they see the person behind the brand.
2. **Consistency is Key**
   Posting regularly helps keep your audience engaged and your presence top of mind. Develop a schedule that works for you and stick to it.
3. **Add Value with Every Post**
   Whether it's inspiration, education, or entertainment,

each piece of content should serve a purpose. Focus on creating posts that resonate with your audience.

4. **Gratitude is Contagious**
   Starting your day with gratitude can set a positive tone for your interactions. Share your gratitude online to inspire others and foster a culture of positivity.
5. **Curate Your Online Space**
   Protect your mental energy by focusing on positivity and growth. Remove negativity and set boundaries for a healthy social media environment.
6. **Leverage Connections for Growth**
   Use social media to connect with like-minded individuals, join study groups, and learn from others' successes. Collaboration and shared knowledge are powerful tools for growth.
7. **Document Your Journey**
   Treat social media as a digital scrapbook—a place to capture the moments that matter and share your story. Your posts are part of the legacy you're building.

Prompt for Reflection

How can you use social media more intentionally to build connections and share your story? Are there opportunities to add more authenticity to your posts or engage with your audience in meaningful ways? What is one small step you could commit to for the next 30 days to move yourself to this goal?

Final Thought

Social media is a platform for connection, inspiration, and storytelling. When used with intention and authenticity, it becomes a tool for building relationships, growing your brand, and leaving a legacy that matters. Embrace its potential, and let your voice make an impact.

Part 3

Taking it from the Minors to the Majors

Chapter 9

Leadership – Lifting Others Up

"A leader is one who knows the way, goes the way, and shows the way."

John C. Maxwell

Leadership is not about titles, positions, or flowcharts. It's about one life influencing another. Over the years, I've come to realize that leadership is one of the most rewarding parts of my career. Watching others succeed and knowing I played a part in their growth has given me purpose far beyond financial success. There's something powerful in lifting others, empowering them to reach new heights, and helping them become leaders in their own right.

Leadership is Influence, Not Authority

When I look back on the individuals I've had the privilege of leading, one thing stands out: leadership is not about being in charge; it's about taking responsibility for those in your charge. Over the years, I've helped four individuals transition into their own agencies—two in Nashville, Tennessee one in Kansas City, Kansas and one in Rock Island, Illinois. Watching them grow from eager team members to successful leaders has been one of my greatest accomplishments.

John Maxwell says it best: “Everything rises and falls on leadership.” If no one is following you, then you're not leading—you're just taking a walk. Influence is the foundation of leadership. It's not about telling people what to do, but about showing them the way through your actions, decisions, and values. True leaders lift others, add value, and inspire people to see beyond their current limitations.

A big part of this influence is not just motivating others to follow but helping them develop a vision for their own success. When I look at the individuals I've mentored, I don't see just a reflection of myself; I see the future potential they carry within them. Leadership is about lighting that spark and helping people realize their own capabilities. It's about handing them the torch, knowing they'll carry it forward with even more strength and wisdom.

Ownership: The Mark of a True Leader

One of the most crucial lessons I've learned in leadership is to own everything. Early on in my career, it was easy to point fingers when things didn't go as planned. But the reality is, as a leader, you have to take responsibility for every outcome—good or bad. It's easy to own the wins, but the true test of leadership comes when you're willing to own the losses too.

In my office, I'm responsible for every decision—from who I hire to how I communicate with the team. The success of the team hinges on my ability to make the right calls, but it also depends on my willingness to learn from the mistakes. Owning both the good and the bad is essential if you want to build trust and respect with your team.

Embrace ownership—accepting both the victories and the failures—I saw my leadership effectiveness skyrocket. Taking ownership shows your team that you're accountable and committed to growth, just like them.

Time is the Greatest Investment

A common misconception about leadership is that it's all about making high-level decisions. While that's part of it, the real impact comes from the time you invest in your team. Your people need you—your guidance, your support, and most importantly, your time. Spending time with your team is how they grow, and it's through that time you show them what leadership really looks like.

When I first started working for Mike Jones back in 2005, I was lucky enough to be mentored in every aspect of the business. Mike didn't just tell me what to do—he showed me. This hands-on approach allowed me to develop the skills I needed to lead my own team later on. As a leader now, I make it a point to invest in my people, not just monetarily but through time and mentorship.

Every hour you spend teaching, guiding, and even listening to your team builds trust. It's the small moments of mentorship, the daily interactions, that lay the groundwork for long-term success. I've always believed that showing up for your team isn't just about being present in the office; it's about being mentally present for each individual on your team.

Cultivating Culture Over Vision

You'll often hear about the importance of vision in leadership—and it's true. You need to know where you're headed, or you'll never get there. But what's even more important is the culture you create. I've always said, "Culture eats vision for lunch." Vision is what you see in the future, but culture is what you're doing every day. It's the daily actions, habits, and values that drive the results in your business.

As a leader, your job is to cultivate that culture. It's not enough to just have a grand vision; you need to create an environment where your team feels supported, valued, and inspired to work towards that vision. That's what separates a good leader from a great one.

In my office, I work hard to create a culture of open communication, learning, and respect. A lot of that starts with my own behavior. You can't expect a positive, hardworking culture if you're not setting the example. Your team watches everything you do. They notice if you're committed, if you're empathetic, and if you're fair. They take their cues from you, so you have to be intentional about the culture you're creating.

Empowering Through Failure

One of the biggest strengths a leader can have is the ability to empower others—even through failure. Failure is part of the process, and if your team isn't failing occasionally, they're not pushing themselves hard enough. I remind my team often that failure is not something to be feared; it's something to embrace. A mentor of mine once shared with me that when someone on his team makes a mistake, he sends them flowers…as a reminder that mistakes are a part of the process of success, he shared he doesn't want his team to be afraid to make mistakes.

Think about the greats like Michael Jordan. He missed a ton of game-winning shots, but he also made the ones that counted. The same applies to leadership. You have to give your team the confidence to take risks, make mistakes, and learn from them. That's how you build a strong, resilient team.

Empowering others to fail doesn't mean letting things fall apart. It means allowing for mistakes within a framework of growth. When your team knows they won't be reprimanded for every misstep, they'll innovate more, work harder, and grow faster. In the long run, that's how great leaders develop other great leaders.

The Power of Listening

Another key aspect of leadership is the ability to listen. Leaders aren't just there to give orders—they're there to learn, grow, and improve alongside their team. A great leader listens to their team's feedback and uses it to make the organization better. It's about creating an open environment where your team feels comfortable sharing their ideas and concerns.

When your team knows you're listening, it builds trust. And trust is the foundation of any successful team. As a leader, I make it a point to stay open to new ideas, no matter how long I've been in the business. There's always room to improve, and often the best ideas come from the people on the front lines.

Listening also means being willing to change. Some of my most important leadership lessons have come from times when I wasn't afraid to listen to feedback and adjust course. Leaders who don't listen often get left behind, as the world around them changes faster than they can adapt.

Leadership is a Lifelong Journey

Leadership doesn't have a finish line. It's a continuous process of growth, learning, and adaptation. You never stop being a leader, and you never stop developing your leadership skills. There's always something new to learn, always room to improve. That's the beauty of leadership—it's a lifelong journey, not a destination.

I've had many leaders in my life who have shaped the way I lead today, but one that stands out is my coach, Terry Amis. He was the toughest coach I ever had, but also the most impactful. He set high expectations and pushed me to my limits. I'll never forget the time he came out to the mound during a high-stakes game and told me, "I believe in you, but you have to believe in yourself." That moment stuck with me, not just in baseball, but in life.

Terry Amis didn't just coach baseball—he coached life. He taught us discipline, perseverance, and the power of belief. That's what leadership is all about—lifting others up and helping them believe in their own potential.

Key Takeaways

1. Leadership is About Lifting Others: True leadership is not about authority but influence. It's about empowering others to succeed and grow, even when they fail.
2. Ownership is Key: A great leader owns both successes and failures. Take responsibility for every outcome, and don't point fingers when things go wrong.

3. Invest Time in Your Team: Leadership requires time. The more time you invest in your team, the more they will grow. Show them the way, don't just tell them.
4. Culture Over Vision: While vision is important, the culture you build is what drives daily results. Focus on creating a supportive, values-driven environment.
5. Failure is Part of the Process: Don't fear failure—embrace it. Encourage your team to take risks, and let them know that failure is a stepping stone to success.
6. Listen to Your Team: The best leaders are great listeners. Create an environment where your team feels comfortable giving feedback and sharing ideas.
7. Leadership is a Lifelong Journey: There's no finish line in leadership. It's a continuous process of learning, growing, and developing.

Prompt for Reflection

Are you investing enough time in your team to help them grow? How can you better cultivate a culture that supports their success, even through failure?

Final Thought

Leadership isn't a destination; it's a journey of lifting others up, empowering them to believe in themselves, and guiding them toward success. Remember, the most impactful leaders are the ones who care, who listen, and who lead by example. Keep leading with purpose—you're changing lives.

Chapter 10

Abundance - A Mindset for Growth

"The only limit to our realization of tomorrow will be our doubts of today."

Franklin D. Roosevelt

One of the biggest differences between people is whether they think with an abundance mindset or a scarcity mindset. This mental gap can shape everything about how someone lives, works, and interacts with the world. In this chapter, I want to explore what it means to live with an abundant mindset, how it contrasts with scarcity thinking, and how you can shift your perspective to embrace abundance in all areas of your life.

A Journey from Scarcity to Abundance

I wasn't always someone who thought with abundance. In fact, early in my life, I had more of a scarcity mindset. It wasn't until I was 25 years old, working as an intern for Rick Brockett in Harrisburg, Illinois, that I began to think differently. Every day, I'd sit in the Subway parking lot, eat the same sandwich, and listen to *The Strangest Secret* by Earl Nightingale. Nightingale's message was clear: *You become what you think about.* Those words, repeated day after day, sparked the beginning of my shift toward an abundant mindset.

Now, at 42, I see the world through a very different lens. But that shift didn't happen overnight. It took time, practice, and a conscious effort to change how I approached risk, opportunity, and failure.

The Scarcity Mindset: Fear of Risk

A scarcity mindset is driven by fear—fear of failure, fear of loss, and fear of risk. Growing up, I heard phrases like "don't get too close to the pond, you might fall in." It's the kind of thinking that says, "Play it safe, don't take risks because something bad might happen."

But here's the truth: failure is a part of success, not the opposite. If you never take risks, you'll never grow, and that's where the scarcity mindset holds you back. A scarcity mindset says, “Don't risk it, because you might fail.” An abundant mindset, on the other hand, says, “Take the risk, because even if you fail, you'll grow.”

You control which mindset you embrace. You can choose to operate from a place of fear and scarcity, or you can choose to see every opportunity as a chance to grow, even if it comes with the possibility of failure. That choice is yours.

Abundance is a Choice

Our brains are naturally wired for survival, which often pushes us toward a scarcity mindset. The world we live in bombards us with messages of limitation, comparison, and fear. But shifting to an abundant mindset requires intentional effort. It's about recognizing that opportunities are limitless, that success is not a zero-sum game, and that you can create your own path.

With an abundance mindset, you stop comparing yourself to others, and you start encouraging them. You realize that there's enough success, enough wealth, and enough opportunity for everyone. You don't need to compete—you can collaborate. You lift others up, share your knowledge freely, and understand that helping others succeed doesn't take anything away from you.

The Role of Money in an Abundant Mindset

For many people, money is the ultimate area where a scarcity mindset prevails. People think, "There's only so much to go around," or "I'll never make more than what I'm earning now." But that's not how money works when you think abundantly. Money is a tool, not a finite resource.

One of the biggest mindset shifts I've made is learning to trade money for time. Time is not abundant. None of us know how much time we have, but money can be used to free up more of it. That's why I choose to pay others to do tasks like mowing the lawn or cleaning the pool. It's not about being lazy; it's about valuing my time and using money to create more freedom for what matters.

Surround Yourself with Abundant Thinkers

Another major key to embracing an abundant mindset is surrounding yourself with people who think the same way. Early in my career, I joined a study group within my company, which helped shape my perspective on abundance. More recently, I joined a mastermind group called *Legacy Family*, which consists of entrepreneurs and real estate investors who think big. These are the kinds of people who believe that if they can dream it, they can do it.

What I love about this group is that there's no competition—only collaboration. Everyone genuinely wants to help each other succeed. There's no jealousy, no comparing, just a group of people lifting each other up and sharing their knowledge. That's the power of an abundant mindset.

If you want to live abundantly, you need to be intentional about the people you surround yourself with. Seek out those who encourage you, who challenge you to grow, and who live with abundance in their own lives.

Jealousy is Poison to Progress

Scarcity thinking breeds jealousy. When you're operating from a scarcity mindset, it's easy to look at others' success and feel envious. But jealousy is poison to your progress. Instead of looking at someone else's accomplishments with envy, look at them with curiosity. Ask yourself, "What can I learn from them? How can I apply their strategies to my own journey?"

People who think abundantly aren't afraid to share their secrets to success. In fact, they're eager to help because they understand that there's enough success to go around. So, instead of feeling jealous, reach out. Ask for advice. Use the resources around you. An abundant thinker sees opportunities for growth, not reasons to be envious.

Don't Compare – Everyone's Journey is Unique

One of the traps of scarcity thinking is comparison. In today's world of social media, it's easy to see someone else's highlight reel and assume their life is perfect. But what you're not seeing is the journey it took to get there—the struggles, the failures, and the sacrifices.

If you're constantly comparing your progress to someone else's, you're missing the point. Everyone's journey is different, and you might be at the beginning of your path while someone else is nearing the peak of theirs. Never compare your chapter one to someone else's chapter 10. Instead of comparing, focus on your own growth, your own journey. Celebrate where you are today, and keep moving forward with an abundant mindset.

The Power of Gratitude and Learning

At the heart of an abundant mindset is gratitude. When you focus on what you already have, rather than what you lack, you create space for more abundance in your life. Gratitude shifts your perspective from scarcity to abundance, reminding you that you're already blessed in so many ways.

In addition to gratitude, abundant thinkers are always learning. They understand that life is a continuous journey of growth, and they're eager to absorb new knowledge, share it with others, and apply it in their own lives. They don't hoard information or resources; they share it freely because they know that abundance isn't about holding on—it's about giving back.

Money: A Tool for Freedom

An abundant mindset sees money as a tool, not as an end goal. Money is a means to create memories with your family, to employ others, to give back, and to live a life of freedom. It's not something to hoard or fear; it's something to use intentionally.

One of the biggest mindset shifts I've experienced with money is learning to value time over cash. When I take my kids to theme parks, we get the fast passes because waiting in long lines is a waste of time. I've worked hard to create a life where I can make choices like that, not because I'm "lucky," but because I've cultivated an abundant mindset.

Abundance in Every Area of Life

An abundant mindset doesn't just apply to money or success—it's a way of seeing the world. It's about believing that there's enough of everything for everyone: enough love, enough opportunity, enough time. When you think abundantly, you see challenges as opportunities and setbacks as setups for a comeback. You start to believe that anything is possible, and that belief shapes your reality.

Key Takeaways

1. **Mindset is Everything:** The difference between scarcity and abundance is all in how you think. Choosing to believe in abundance opens up new possibilities and opportunities.
2. **Abundance Starts with Gratitude:** Focusing on what you already have creates a foundation for more blessings to flow into your life.
3. **Surround Yourself with Abundance:** The people you spend time with influence your mindset. Choose to be around those who encourage growth, collaboration, and positivity.

4. **Money is a Tool, Not a Goal:** An abundant thinker sees money as a tool for freedom, experiences, and making a positive impact.
5. **Avoid Comparison:** Everyone's journey is unique. Focus on your own growth and progress instead of comparing yourself to others.
6. **Embrace Learning:** Never stop learning. An abundant mindset thrives on curiosity, growth, and the willingness to share knowledge.

Prompt for Reflection

Are there areas where you've been holding back due to fear or scarcity thinking? How can you shift your mindset toward abundance in your daily life?

Final Thought

Living with an abundant mindset means embracing the idea that there's more than enough for everyone. It's about believing in possibility, lifting others up, and seeing opportunities where others see limitations. Let abundance guide your actions, and watch how it transforms your life.

Chapter 11

Coaching

An Investment in Transformation

"A coach is someone who tells you what you don't want to hear, who has you see what you don't want to see, so you can be who you have always known you could be."

Tom Landry

For years, I resisted the idea of hiring a professional coach. I attended study groups, networked with high-achievers who raved about the benefits of coaching, and admired their results. Yet, I held back, unsure if the cost would be worth the investment. But sometimes, the universe gives you exactly what you need at the right time.

In 2023, business challenges began to weigh heavily on me, pushing me into uncharted mental territory. During a casual lunch, a colleague suggested I meet Jason Hietbrink, a professional coach who had significantly impacted his own life. Skeptical yet intrigued, I accepted the offer for a ession. That one call changed everything.

Hiring Jason as my coach was one of the biggest financial investments I've ever made in myself—$30,000 to be exact. It wasn't an easy decision, but in hindsight, it has been worth every penny. Coaching isn't just about improving business performance; it's about redefining who you are, aligning your actions with your values, and achieving clarity in ways you never imagined.

Rediscovering Identity

One of the first exercises Jason guided me through was deceptively simple yet profound. He asked me a question that stopped me in my tracks: *"Who are you?"* I instinctively started listing my achievements, roles, and responsibilities: "I'm one of the top insurance agents, a dedicated father, a hard worker…" He cut me off: *"I didn't ask what you do. I asked who you are."*

That question forced me to reflect deeply. Beneath the titles and accomplishments, I realized I had lost sight of my true self. I had tied my identity so tightly to external validation—trophies, accolades, and daily production—that I forgot who I was at my core. This realization was both humbling and liberating.

Through coaching, I began to separate my sense of self from my achievements. Jason helped me see that I didn't need to "win" every day to feel worthy. He guided me to reconnect with the fun-loving, driven, and passionate person I've always been, regardless of professional success.

The Power of Clarity

One of Jason's most impactful exercises involved creating a simple T-chart. On one side, I listed everything I wanted in life; on the other, everything I didn't have but desired. This exercise illuminated how much of what I wanted, I already had.

The clarity I gained from this exercise was transformative. It shifted my focus from scarcity to abundance and helped me identify priorities that truly mattered—my family, health, and peace of mind. It also revealed the distractions and energy vampires that were draining me.

Jason introduced me to the concept of an energy audit, another T-chart exercise where I listed activities, thoughts and beliefs, that brought positive energy versus those that drained me. Identifying these energy dynamics was eye-opening. By addressing the sources of negativity, I was able to protect my mental space and cultivate a more fulfilling day-to-day life.

Shifting the Scoreboard

Before coaching, I measured success primarily by daily production numbers and annual goals. While metrics are essential in any business, they had begun to dictate my happiness. Jason challenged me to redefine my scoreboard.

Instead of focusing solely on financial success, I started tracking time spent with loved ones, personal growth milestones, and overall net worth as a long-term measure of success. This shift allowed me to prioritize what truly mattered and align my actions with my values.

Through this process, I realized that saying “family comes first” wasn’t enough—I had to live it. Coaching helped me bridge the gap between my intentions and my actions, ensuring that my priorities were reflected in how I spent my time and energy.

The Cost of Growth

Coaching required sacrifices—time, money, and comfort. But it also taught me to establish non-negotiables in my life. Jason asked me two critical questions:

1. What are you willing to sacrifice to achieve greatness?

2. What are you *not* willing to sacrifice?

These questions forced me to draw clear boundaries. While I was willing to sacrifice certain comforts to grow my business, I was unwilling to compromise my relationships, health, or integrity. Defining these boundaries brought clarity to my decision-making and ensured I stayed true to my values.

Accountability and Gratitude

One of the most valuable lessons from coaching was the importance of accountability. Jason encouraged me to involve my children in this process, making them my accountability partners. I shared my goals with them and invited their feedback if I veered off track—like spending too much time on my phone or not being present during family moments.

This exercise not only improved my habits but also deepened my relationship with my kids. It showed them that growth is a lifelong journey and that it's okay to seek help along the way.

Jason also emphasized the importance of gratitude. By focusing on the present and appreciating what I already have, I was able to find joy in the journey rather than constantly chasing the next achievement.

Why Everyone Needs a Coach

Coaching isn't just for athletes or business leaders—it's for anyone who wants to unlock their potential. A great coach sees what you can't, challenges you to grow, and holds you accountable.

If Michael Jordan, one of the greatest basketball players of all time, relied on a coach, why shouldn't we? Coaching provides an objective perspective and a structured approach to tackling challenges, both personal and professional.

Investing in a coach was one of the best decisions I've ever made. It has transformed how I approach my business, relationships, and personal development. If you're considering hiring a coach, my advice is simple: don't wait until it feels financially comfortable. The returns on investing in yourself far outweigh the costs.

Final Thoughts

Coaching isn't a quick fix—it's a journey of self-discovery, accountability, and growth. It requires vulnerability, hard work, and a willingness to change. But the rewards are immeasurable.

Whether you're struggling with clarity, seeking balance, or simply aiming for the next level, a coach can help you get there. Remember, the best investment you can make is in yourself.

Takeaways

1. **Know Who You Are, Beyond What You Do**
   Rediscovering your identity is crucial. Achievements and accolades don't define you—your core values, passions, and relationships do. Reflect on who you are at your essence, separate from your roles or titles.
2. **Clarity Brings Focus**
   Exercises like the T-chart and energy audit help prioritize what truly matters while identifying and eliminating energy-draining activities. Focus on what fuels you and aligns with your goals.
3. **Redefine Success**
   Shift your metrics of success from daily or annual achievements to lifelong impact and values. Celebrate time spent with loved ones, personal growth, and meaningful progress over external validation.
4. **Set Non-Negotiables**
   Clearly define what you are and aren't willing to sacrifice. These boundaries ensure you grow in ways that align with your principles and protect what's most important.

5. **Invest in Accountability**
   Sharing your goals and inviting feedback from loved ones fosters growth and strengthens relationships. Accountability doesn't just come from coaches—it comes from the people who matter most.
6. **Gratitude Transforms Perspective**
   Appreciating what you already have shifts your mindset from scarcity to abundance. Living in the present allows you to find joy and fulfillment in the journey.
7. **Coaching Is for Everyone**
   A great coach challenges you, provides clarity, and holds you accountable. If even the greatest athletes need coaches, so do we. Invest in yourself—it's worth it.

Prompt for Reflection

- Who are you, at your core, beyond your achievements and roles?
- What activities or relationships drain your energy, and how can you address them?
- Are your actions aligned with your priorities? If not, what needs to change?

Final Thought

The journey to self-improvement isn't easy, but it's worth every step. A coach can help you uncover your potential, stay accountable, and create a life aligned with your values. Don't wait to invest in yourself—the best version of you is waiting.

Chapter 12

Legacy

Building a Ripple Effect

"Legacy is not leaving something for people. It's leaving something in people."

Peter Strople

Legacy is one of those words that carries weight—it's not just about what you leave behind, but the impact you make while you're here. For me, legacy is less about wealth or possessions and more about how you show up for others, the lessons you instill, and the ripple effect of your actions. Every conversation, every decision, every relationship has the potential to leave a mark far greater than we can imagine.

Defining Legacy: Beyond Material Possessions

When most people hear the word "legacy," their minds jump to material wealth—houses, businesses, or money left behind for family and future generations. But legacy is about so much more than tangible assets. It's about the intangible—the values, habits, and mindset that influence others long after you're gone.

One of the most profound lessons I've learned is that legacy begins with how you live your life today. It's in the everyday actions, the consistency in showing up for those around you, and the impact you make, no matter how small. For me, legacy isn't just what I leave for my kids—it's what I leave in them. It's about teaching them how to dream big, work hard, and approach life with a heart full of gratitude.

The Ripple Effect of Leadership

Throughout my career, I've seen firsthand how leadership and legacy go hand in hand. True leadership isn't about being in charge or having all the answers—it's about empowering others to succeed. It's about creating a ripple effect where the people you touch go on to impact others.

Take, for example, my role in coaching at Iconic Elite, a basketball program where I volunteer my time to mentor young athletes and their coaches. It's not a paid position, but the rewards are invaluable. The kids in this program often come from challenging backgrounds, and for many of them, basketball is more than a game—it's an outlet, a source of confidence, and a pathway to opportunities.

By investing in these kids, I'm helping to build a legacy of resilience, teamwork, and determination. They might not remember every game we've played or every drill we've practiced, but they will carry the lessons of discipline and belief in themselves for the rest of their lives.

Family First: The Foundation of Legacy

While my professional pursuits are a big part of my life, my family is at the heart of everything I do. My legacy begins at home—with my children, Hudson and Lola. It's about teaching them to see the world through a lens of abundance, to lead with kindness, and to embrace challenges as opportunities for growth.

Every moment spent with my kids is an opportunity to instill values that will guide them throughout their lives. Whether it's cheering them on at basketball games or sitting down for dinner together, these moments create memories that shape their understanding of love, support, and perseverance.

The Role of Intentionality in Legacy Building

Legacy doesn't happen by accident—it requires intentionality. Every decision you make, every action you take, contributes to the story you're writing. It's about being deliberate in how you spend your time, where you invest your energy, and who you surround yourself with.

Intentionality also means looking beyond the present moment and considering the long-term impact of your choices. For me, that's why I'm so passionate about financial planning and life insurance. It's not just about protecting assets; it's about protecting futures. It's about ensuring that the people you care about are taken care of, no matter what.

Giving Back: A Legacy of Service

One of the most rewarding aspects of my journey has been the ability to give back to my community. Whether it's through mentoring young athletes, supporting local initiatives, or simply being present for someone in need, service is a cornerstone of my legacy.

Service isn't always about grand gestures—it's about the small, consistent actions that show people they matter. It's about listening, showing up, and being a source of encouragement. The impact of these actions often goes far beyond what we can see in the moment.

Leaving a Legacy of Growth

Growth is an essential component of legacy. It's about continuously striving to be better so that you can pour into others. Growth isn't just about professional achievements—it's about personal development, learning from your experiences, and using those lessons to make a difference.

For me, growth means waking up every day with a mindset of gratitude and a determination to make the most of the opportunities in front of me. It means setting goals, taking action, and never settling for mediocrity. It's about leaving a legacy that inspires others to dream bigger and reach higher.

A Legacy That Lasts

At the end of the day, legacy isn't about what you accumulate—it's about what you contribute. It's about the lives you touch, the lessons you teach, and the memories you create. When I think about my own legacy, I want to be remembered as someone who lived with purpose, who served others, and who inspired those around me to be their best selves.

Legacy isn't something you start building at the end of your life—it's something you build every single day. It's in the way you treat people, the effort you put into your passions, and the values you pass on to the next generation. It's about leaving the world a little better than you found it.

Let's get to work on building a legacy that truly matters.

Takeaways

1. **Legacy Is More Than Material**: Legacy goes beyond wealth or possessions—it's about the values, memories, and impact you leave behind for those around you.
2. **The Ripple Effect of Leadership**: True leadership creates a ripple effect, inspiring others to grow and succeed. Empowering others to lead amplifies your legacy far beyond what you can achieve alone.
3. **Family as the Foundation**: Building a legacy starts at home. Every moment spent with your family is an opportunity to instill values and create lasting memories.
4. **Intentionality Is Key**: Legacy doesn't happen by chance—it requires deliberate choices, thoughtful actions, and a long-term perspective.

5. **Service Builds Significance**: Serving others through small, consistent actions makes a difference that lasts a lifetime. It's not about what you do for recognition but about the lives you touch.
6. **Growth Fuels Legacy**: Personal and professional growth ensures you're continuously evolving into the person capable of leaving a meaningful impact.

Prompt for Reflection

What does legacy mean to you? Look over your calendar for the past two weeks, is how you are investing your time and energy align with the legacy you want to leave?

Final Thought

Legacy isn't about what you leave for people—it's about what you leave in them. By living with purpose, serving others, and striving for growth, you can create a ripple effect that extends far beyond your lifetime. Start building your legacy today, one intentional action at a time.

Conclusion

Embracing the Journey, A Life of Purpose, Persistence, and Growth

---

"Success is not measured by the position one has reached in life, but by the obstacles one has overcome while trying to succeed."

Booker T. Washington

As we close this book, let's take a moment to reflect on the path we've traveled together. From understanding the power of vision to embracing the value of perseverance, adaptability, and purpose, each chapter has offered tools, insights, and practical steps toward creating a life that's not only successful but also fulfilling. Life and business are unpredictable, filled with both victories and challenges, and how you navigate them defines your journey. This journey isn't just about the destinations you reach but about the growth, resilience, and strength you build along the way.

Success is a deeply personal journey. It's not a one-size-fits-all blueprint but rather a path you carve out through experience, dedication, and the courage to keep going, no matter the obstacles. In many ways, this journey reflects the core qualities of those who achieve lasting fulfillment. In these final pages, let's revisit some of the core principles that will guide you forward, empowering you to live a life marked by growth, resilience, and an unwavering commitment to your values and vision.

The Power of Vision: Knowing Where You're Headed

One of the most critical aspects of success is having a clear vision. Vision acts as your compass, guiding you toward your goals and reminding you why you started in the first place. Throughout this book, we've emphasized the importance of having a purpose-driven vision, one that aligns with your values and aspirations. But having a vision is more than just setting goals—it's about creating a life that reflects who you are and who you want to become.

A compelling vision is what pulls you forward when challenges arise. It's the reason you get up every day, ready to take on the world, even when the path is uncertain. But remember, your vision doesn't have to be rigid. Life will throw unexpected twists and turns your way, and sometimes, your vision may evolve. Be open to these shifts and allow your vision to grow alongside you. Embrace change as a natural part of the journey, knowing that each pivot brings new opportunities for learning and growth.

Building Resilience: The Courage to Continue

Resilience is the fuel that powers your journey, especially during challenging times. As we've explored, resilience isn't about avoiding difficulties but rather about facing them head-on, learning from them, and growing stronger. Every setback you encounter is an opportunity to develop resilience, to prove to yourself that you're capable of overcoming anything that stands in your way.

Life will test your resilience in countless ways. Sometimes, you'll face setbacks that make you question your path. In these moments, remember the importance of persistence—the courage to continue, even when giving up feels easier. Each time you choose resilience, you're building a foundation that will support you in every aspect of life. Resilience is the heart of true strength, enabling you to bounce back, adapt, and move forward with a renewed sense of purpose.

Embracing Change: Adaptability as a Pathway to Growth

The ability to adapt is essential for long-term success. The world around us is constantly evolving, and those who thrive are those who can adjust, pivot, and find new ways forward. Adaptability isn't just about reacting to change; it's about embracing it as a chance to grow. In the face of uncertainty, adaptability allows you to maintain your course, even when the landscape shifts.

Being adaptable also means staying curious and open to new ideas. As we discussed, continuous learning fuels adaptability. When you're committed to growth and open to change, you'll find that every experience, whether positive or challenging, adds to your knowledge and resilience. Cultivating adaptability means letting go of rigid expectations and trusting that each turn in the road is guiding you closer to where you're meant to be.

Purpose and Passion: Fuel for the Journey

Purpose gives meaning to everything you do. It's what transforms ordinary actions into powerful steps toward a life of fulfillment. As we've explored, having a purpose that resonates deeply with you is essential for staying motivated, especially when times get tough. Purpose is the "why" behind your actions, the reason you continue to push forward, even when the path feels difficult.

Finding and embracing your purpose is one of the most rewarding aspects of life. Purpose isn't just about the impact you make on others; it's about creating a life that aligns with your values and passions. When you're driven by purpose, every challenge becomes more manageable, every success more meaningful. Remember, purpose isn't always something you discover overnight. It can evolve over time, shaped by your experiences, growth, and self-discovery.

Consistency: The Key to Lasting Success

Consistency is often the unsung hero of success. It's the small, repeated actions that build momentum and drive long-term progress. Whether it's maintaining your daily habits, setting aside time for personal growth, or staying disciplined in your goals, consistency creates a foundation that supports every other element of success.

In this journey, there will be days when motivation feels low and distractions abound. On these days, consistency becomes your anchor. It's the commitment to show up, even when you don't feel like it, that separates those who achieve lasting success from those who fall short. Consistency turns vision into reality, and it's often the difference between dreaming of success and actually achieving it.

Surrounding Yourself with the Right People

Success is not a solo journey. The people you surround yourself with play a significant role in your growth and success. Throughout this book, we've touched on the importance of building a support system of mentors, friends, and colleagues who encourage, challenge, and uplift you. These relationships are invaluable—they provide perspective, guidance, and inspiration when you need it most.

Seek out people who align with your values and share your vision for growth. A strong support system isn't just about having people who cheer you on; it's about surrounding yourself with individuals who challenge you to become your best self. The right people will help you stay focused, hold you accountable, and remind you of your potential, even when self-doubt creeps in.

Celebrating Progress: Finding Joy in the Journey

As you pursue your goals, it's easy to become fixated on the destination, to focus solely on what's next. But remember, success is not just about reaching a specific endpoint; it's about enjoying the journey, celebrating the progress you make along the way. Each small win, each lesson learned, and each step forward is worth acknowledging.

Celebrating progress keeps you motivated and reminds you that success is a journey, not a final destination. Take time to reflect on how far you've come, to appreciate the growth you've experienced, and to recognize the resilience you've built. Success is a series of moments, each one adding to the richness of your journey. Embrace these moments—they're what make the pursuit worthwhile.

The Legacy of a Life Well-Lived

As you move forward, remember that success is not just about personal achievements; it's about the impact you leave on others and the legacy you create. A life of purpose, resilience, adaptability, and growth inspires those around you, leaving a mark that extends beyond individual accomplishments. When you lead by example, you pave the way for others to pursue their own paths with courage and conviction.

Consider the legacy you want to leave behind. How do you want to be remembered? What values do you want to pass on to future generations? Success isn't just about what you accomplish; it's about who you become along the way and the positive influence you have on the lives you touch.

Moving Forward with Confidence

As you close this book and take the lessons with you, know that you're equipped to face any challenge, seize any opportunity, and create a life that reflects your deepest values and aspirations. Success is within reach, but it's up to you to take the steps, to persevere, to adapt, and to stay true to your purpose. The journey may not always be easy, but it will be filled with growth, discovery, and moments of profound fulfillment.

Embrace each challenge as an opportunity, each setback as a stepping stone, and each victory as a reminder of your strength. The path ahead is yours to shape, and with the right mindset, vision, and determination, there's nothing you cannot achieve. Remember, the true measure of success isn't found in the destination but in the journey itself. Go forward with confidence, knowing that you have the power to create a life of meaning, impact, and lasting success.

Made in the USA
Columbia, SC
03 June 2025

58863676R00080